My debt to history is one which
cannot be calculated. I know of no other
motivation which so accounts for my
awakening interest as a young lad in the
principles of leadership and government. . . .
I know that the one great external influence
which, more than anything else,
nourished and sustained that interest in
government and public service was the endless
reading of history which I began as a boy
and which I have kept up ever since.

HARRY TRUMAN

The unparalleled rise of America
has not been the result of riches in lands,
forests, or mines; it sprang from
the ideas and ideals which liberated minds
and stimulated the spirits of men.
In those ideas and ideals are the soul
of the people. No American can
review this vast pageant of progress without
confidence and faith, without courage, strength,
and resolution for the future.

HERBERT HOOVER

Kennedy: "A Nation of Immigrants," New York, 1959
Eisenhower: Reader's Digest, October, 1948
Truman: "Memoirs," © 1955, Time Inc.
Hoover: 150th anniversary address, Yorktown, Va., October 19, 1931

Important Dates and Events to Remember
986-1701

986 Bjarni Heriulfsson blown off course en route to Greenland is first white man to view North American continent.

1000 Leif the Lucky leaves Greenland, spends three years exploring lands from northern Maine to southern Massachusetts.

1492 October 12, Columbus lands in the Bahamas, discovers America for Spain.

1497 July, John Cabot returns to England after an unsuccessful search for a northwest passage. His explorations permit England to claim her navigators were first on continent of North America. Amerigo Vespucci, makes first of four voyages to New World.

1506 May 20, Christopher Columbus dies, having returned three times to the newfound lands, never realizing he has discovered a new world.

1507 Map of the New World appears. It names South America for Amerigo Vespucci.

1513 Vasco Núñez de Balboa crosses Panama, discovers and claims the Pacific.

1521 Hernando Cortés captures Mexico.

1522 Ships of Ferdinand Magellan complete circumnavigation of the earth.

1524 Giovanni da Verrazano believed to have sailed up the Hudson River, giving rise to "bird from heaven" Indian legend.

1528 Alvar Núñez Cabeza de Vaca and party of 250 men are shipwrecked near Galveston, Texas. Surviving few explore Southwest, learn of Seven Cities of Gold.

1534 April 20, Jacques Cartier sails in search of a northwest passage, explores the St. Lawrence River, and establishes first French claims to New World.

1539 Spring, Hernando de Soto lands with 620 men at Charlotte Bay, Florida.

1540 Francisco Vásquez de Coronado finds Seven Cities of Gold—a Zuñi village glittering in the sunlight.

1541 Spring, de Soto discovers the Mississippi River, but dies soon after of malaria.

1542 Juan Rodriguez Cabrillo discovers Santa Monica Bay, three islands of Santa Barbara, and San Diego Bay in the name of Spain.

1565 First permanent settlement in the New World is founded by Spaniards at St. Augustine, Florida.

1579 Francis Drake, during three-year trip around the world, claims California for the English queen.

1583 Sir Humphrey Gilbert on second voyage to the New World takes possession of Newfoundland for England.

1585 June, Sir Richard Grenville lands colonists on Roanoke Island.

1587 Virginia Dare is first child of English parents born in North America.

1603 Samuel de Champlain explores St. Lawrence River to rapids above Montreal.

1607 Virginia Company launches English colony at Jamestown.

1608 Champlain founds the first white settlement in Canada, at Quebec.

1609 Henry Hudson sails up Hudson River.

1613-14 Adriaen Block discovers Housatonic and Connecticut Rivers, Rhode Island and Block Island.

1619 First Negro slaves brought to Virginia. First legislative body meets in America.

1620 September 6, some one hundred Pilgrims crowd aboard the *Mayflower* bound for Virginia to seek religious freedom. On November 11, after a stormy voyage, they sight land. The Mayflower Compact is drawn up and signed by all male passengers. In December, a settlement is founded at Plymouth.

1621 November, a good harvest is celebrated with the first Thanksgiving.

1623 Dutch West India Company, chartered two years earlier, brings first Dutch settlers to America—some settle at Nassau (now Albany), some on Governor's Island, in New York Bay.

1626 Peter Minuit purchases Ma-na-hat-ta Island from the Indians for about $24. Dutch settlement is founded there and called "New Amsterdam."

1630 Puritans of Massachusetts Bay Company found Boston as their chief settlement.

1630-40 Great migration of English to America creates new towns.

1633 Dissatisfied with Puritan codes, many leave Massachusetts to resettle in fertile lands along the Connecticut River.

1634 Catholic and Protestant settle together in St. Marys, Maryland, realizing Lord Baltimore's dream of a colony with religious freedom.

1636 Harvard College becomes first institution of higher learning in America. Roger Williams, banished from the colony by the General Court of Massachusetts for religious liberalism, founds a colony at Providence, Rhode Island.

1637 A band of Pequot braves ambush citizens of Wethersfield. By order of the General Court of Connecticut, a militia is organized, and English settlers and Indians fight for American land for the first time.

1638 Peter Minuit organizes first Swedish colony at present site of Wilmington, Delaware.

1639 First "post office" is established in Boston by General Court of Massachusetts. Connecticut adopts Fundamental Orders, colonies' first written constitution.

1640 *Bay Psalm Book* becomes the first book printed in America.

1642 General Court of Massachusetts orders parents to teach their children to read and write. Later, in 1647, it requires townships of fifty families or more to support a school.

1649 "Act Concerning Religion" granting religious freedom is passed by General Assembly in Maryland.

1658 New England Confederation denies Quakers right to worship in its colonies.

1664 August, British warships demand the Dutch surrender New Amsterdam. Under British rule, the city is renamed "New York."

1673 Father Marquette and Louis Joliet explore the Mississippi River as far as the mouth of the Arkansas River.

1682 April 9, Robert Cavelier, Sieur de la Salle reaches the mouth of the Mississippi River and claims the lands drained by its tributaries as well as a large part of the coast of the Gulf of Mexico for France. He calls this territory Louisiana. Autumn, Quaker William Penn comes to America. At Shackamaxon, near Philadelphia, he makes a treaty of amnesty with the Indians for lands the Quakers are to colonize. Later Philadelphia becomes the new province's capital.

1690 Although it lasts only one issue, *Publick Occurrences*, printed in Boston, becomes the colonies' first newspaper.

1701 Frenchmen found Detroit, after having discovered the lands bordering on the Great Lakes.

INTRODUCTION

To you, as an American boy or girl, history is the story of why you feel, and think, and act the way you do. Long years ago other youngsters like yourself awoke in the morning—glad when they beheld a beaming sun, drowsy when they heard the beat of rain on the roof, gloomy when threatening clouds gathered overhead—but a new day still budged them out of bed.

For being alive was what counted. Going to school, coming home, growing up were wonderful adventures. We can date the age when George Washington or Andrew Jackson or Abraham Lincoln grew from boyhood into manhood, but that fact isn't too important. They were like you, these youngsters of former years—not knowing that they were actors in history, but simply hoping that somehow, despite all their inner doubts, they would make a go of the years ahead.

And of course they did—as you will. Better than any other source, history reveals this truth to us. Great events grow out of average people like you and me—people who do what they think they should, who cling to their own principles and ideals, and who call by the name of freedom their right to do so.

The Golden Book History of the United States begins a long time ago—in the year 986 A.D. A great many people—some noble, some mean—walk through its pages. Each has something to tell us. Each is somehow part of ourselves. I hope that you will have the same fun I did in making this discovery.

EARL SCHENCK MIERS

THE GOLDEN BOOK

HISTORY of the

UNITED STATES

by **EARL SCHENCK MIERS**

LITT. B., M. A., L. H. D.

VOLUME
1
THE EXPLORERS

Paintings by **ALTON S. TOBEY**

Drawings by **RICHARD P. KLUGA**

Technical Consultants:
L. ETHAN ELLIS AND RICHARD M. BROWN
of the Department of History, Rutgers University

HERBERT J. SANBORN, *Art Research*

GOLDEN PRESS · **NEW YORK**

How To Use This Volume THE EXPLORERS tells the story of the discovery and exploration of America from A.D. 986 to 1701, and may be read from cover to cover. It discusses many events that took place over a long span of time. The events taken up in each chapter are described briefly at the opening of the chapter and also on the contents page. This will allow the reader to find any subject he wants quickly and easily. Each section of the text also has the dates of the period it covers printed in blue at the top of the page. The principal events and the dates on which they occurred are listed in the timetable on the inside front cover. Maps are included throughout the text, and also on the inside back cover. An index for the entire series is contained in Volume X.

CONTENTS ~ THE EXPLORERS

Library of Congress Catalog Card Number: 63-9433

© Copyright 1963 by Golden Press, Inc. and The Ridge Press, Inc. Printed in the U.S.A. by Western Printing and Lithographing Co.

Designed and produced by
The Ridge Press, Inc.
17 East 45th Street, New York, N.Y.

LEIF THE LUCKY SAILS TO NORTH AMERICA

Bold Norsemen set out from Greenland and explore the coast of an unknown land, but their discovery of North America is forgotten.

A thousand years ago no voyager wanted to sail beyond the sight of land, for dark mystery haunted the open sea. No matter how carefully a navigator set his course, skies could blacken with an unexpected storm. Then rain fell, lightning flashed, thunder grumbled, and towering waves rose like walls around ship and crew. Equally dangerous, a cold night might be followed by a warm morning. At such times fog dropped like a curtain over the water and the winds grew still. In the silence, the sailors pulled on creaking oars. Cautiously their little ships edged ahead.

Leif the Lucky

In the year 986 A.D., Bjarni Heriulfsson, a brave Norseman, left Iceland to join his father in Greenland. Even though Bjarni [pronounced By-arni] never before had sailed these icy seas, old hands at the voyage told him not to worry. Cape Farewell, the

Routes followed by Bjarni Heriulfsson and Leif the Lucky long before Columbus' voyage

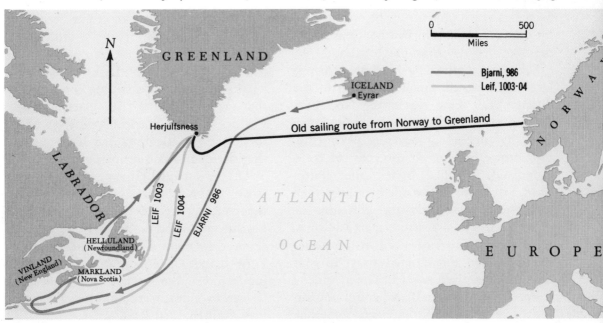

Wheat and grapes were found in the new land.

after the year 1000, Bjarni told his tale to Leif the Lucky, son of famous old Eric the Red. Eager to see this strange land, Leif Ericson begged his father to go with him, for old Eric was the best navigator in the northern seas. Had he not, years ago, won fame as the discoverer of Greenland? Eric shook his head. He was too old now to attempt such an adventure. But Leif was young and strong. Go, Eric told his son. Seek your fame and fortune.

Leif bought a ship from Bjarni and engaged a crew of thirty-five men and women. One was a strange short fellow with a protruding forehead, a small face, and restless eyes. He was Tyrker, a German who had known Leif since childhood and was like a foster father to him. Next to Eric, Leif loved no man so much as Tyrker.

LEIF THE LUCKY EXPLORES THE NEW WORLD

Leif the Lucky left Greenland with strong winds filling the sails of his boat. Straight as an arrow he voyaged to the new country beyond the North Atlantic. His first sight of land was a bleak coast of many ice mountains (probably Labrador or northern Newfoundland) and from the word *hellur*, meaning large flat stones, he gave the place the name of "Helluland." In a small boat a party went ashore, shivering in the breezes that swept down from the glaciers. There was not a single blade of grass on which to feed the cattle they had brought, and they decided to sail to the south.

The next land Leif saw may have been Cape Breton Island or Nova Scotia. Here the country was level and wooded, the beaches white and sandy, and Leif gave the country the name of "Markland," meaning Forest Land. Once more they set sail, seeking regions Bjarni had not described. Driven by a northeast wind, after two days they again sighted land.

southern point of Greenland, could be seen halfway across the sea from Iceland.

For three days, under fair winds, Bjarni and his crew skimmed over the waves toward Greenland. Then all at once the winds died away. That night, all next day, and the day that followed, fog settled over the water. No one knows for certain how many days Bjarni drifted, but long after he had expected to reach Greenland, he was still on the open sea. At last the weather cleared and the following day Bjarni sighted land.

Bjarni now approached a shore that was level and wooded. Small hills rose in the distance. For some reason the Norsemen did not land, although they could not know then that instead of reaching Greenland, they probably were off the coast of Newfoundland. Mystified, Bjarni sailed northward, first past a flat wooded country, then on to shores above which rose glistening ice mountains. The first white man known to have found the continent of North America simply looked and hurried away. In four days Bjarni arrived safely in Greenland.

Years went by, but Bjarni could not forget the new country he had seen. Sometime

Today no one can say for certain exactly where the Norsemen went ashore. But we do know that Leif and his followers landed upon an island somewhere along the Atlantic coast between northern Maine and southern Massachusetts. There was dew on the grass. When they touched moistened fingers to their mouths, the dew seemed sweeter than any they ever had tasted. They sailed across a sound to another strip of land, and Leif sent the swiftest runners in his party to explore the unknown countryside. These scouts, legend says, were a man and a woman, dressed in a kind of plaid and kilt such as Scottish Highlanders wear. They returned after two and a half days, with a cluster of wild grapes and a sheaf of wheat.

Although Norse ships were small, they were sturdy and seaworthy.

Leif decided to build dwellings and to spend the approaching winter in this land of the sweet dew. He sailed to an island where so many eiderducks nested the Norsemen found it impossible to step between the eggs. They discovered a river flowing into a lake where hundreds of salmon leaped in the water. Tall grasses supplied excellent food for the cattle, and close by were hillsides to shelter their huts. The year was 1003 A.D.

One day Tyrker the German—Leif's beloved foster father—was missing. Twelve men were sent to search for him, but soon Tyrker returned, shouting that he had come upon hundreds of wild grapevines.

Leif embraced his old friend. He ordered the grapes gathered and dried so that they could be carried home. With the coming of the spring the ship was loaded and Leif set sail for Greenland. So ended the adventure of the first white men and women to dwell in North America.

THE NORSEMEN ABANDON AMERICA

The following year Leif's brother, Thorvald, visited the same land and found the winter dwellings that Leif had built. After this party left, other Norsemen visited these lands. Then mystery once more closed like a fog over the vast continent of North America. Almost five centuries passed, and not another white man appeared on the sandy beaches where Leif the Lucky had made his home.

Columbus used an astrolabe, like the one at right, to calculate his position at sea.

THE WORLD AWAKENS

As Europe learns more about the world, navigators seek new routes to the treasures of Asia. Columbus plans a voyage to the Orient.

In this age of jet planes that soar across the ocean in a few hours, it is difficult to imagine how much smaller was the world of a thousand years ago. If you had lived in Europe then, the chances are that from birth to death you would never have traveled more than a dozen miles from your home. Everything you needed to exist would be produced in the town or manor of your birth—all the food you ate, the simple clothes you wore, the crude tools you used. If by luck you had been born a lord, you would have spent your time hunting or jousting or carrying on small wars over boundaries and hunting rights with the owners of neighboring manors. You would have administered the affairs of your castle, conducted its religious life, and depended for your own food upon the labors of the many who were your humble serfs (slaves).

Gradually, however, there came a change, especially in the towns along the sea. Ships appeared from strange lands, bringing war at first, but in time bringing trade. Behind the walls of these growing towns a new class of people called merchants began to appear. In the open squares of the town, daily or weekly markets were held. To acquire goods with which to barter, farmers increased the products they grew. Weavers of cloth, or carpenters, or makers of candles, among others, began to give the world its first manufactures. Men from western Europe, journeying into distant lands, learned from the Moslems new ideas about food and clothing and customs. What a wonder it must have been for the first time to touch materials like muslin or damask, to discover the taste of rice or sugar, of lemons or apricots, or of food seasoned with garlic!

By the time the year 1300 arrived, traders and missionaries, crossing overland to many parts of Asia, had made the world a much bigger, more exciting place in which to live. From the Orient came new wonders: precious stones, fabrics of cotton and silk, rugs, glassware, perfume, dyes, ivory, medicines, spices. Europeans worked longer hours to produce articles of trade: woolen fabrics, wines, furs, sulphur, oil, honey, grain. Travelers told of cities with walls of silver and palaces with roofs of gold. Marco Polo told stories of his fabulous adventures in the strange, mysterious kingdoms of Asia. For the first time Europeans learned of life behind the Great Wall in China. They learned, too, of the islands in the Pacific called Japan, Java, and Sumatra, and of remote regions in Siberia where men traveled by dogsled and rode reindeer.

Christopher Columbus

PORTUGUESE SAILORS EXPLORE THE COAST OF AFRICA

Prince Henry the Navigator of Portugal set up a school for the study of geography and navigation. When he died in 1460, his ships had sailed along two thousand miles of the coast of Africa. Portugal grew wealthy on the gold, ivory, and slaves its sailors found in these jungle lands. Map makers were kept busy charting the new trade routes. The invention of instruments like the compass and astrolabe enabled navigators to set their courses with greater accuracy. Some educated men began to believe that the world was round. If that were true, a ship sailing due west should be able to reach the Orient.

At this time, a boy named Christopher Columbus was growing up in Genoa. The son of a weaver, by day he helped his father at the loom. In the evening he listened

The oldest globe in existence was made in 1491 by Martin Behaim. Coming before the journey of Columbus, it does not show America.

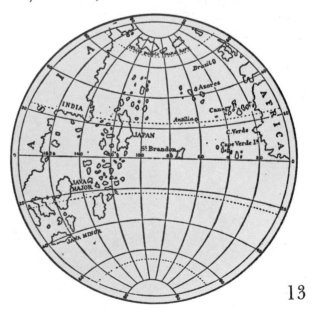

13

eagerly to the exciting tales told by the sailors at the wharves. He longed to go to sea, and he taught himself Latin because that was the language in which all the books on geography were written.

He read and dreamed and awaited his chance. It came when he was about nineteen. He signed aboard a Genoese galley seeking a crew to fight pirates off the Barbary coast of northern Africa.

The more Columbus sailed the sea, the more he loved the life he had chosen. He learned to reef a sail, to steer, to measure distance by eye, to recognize the signs of approaching storms. On one voyage off the coast of Portugal, the Genoese ships with which he was sailing were attacked by a French and Portuguese fleet. Sailors drowned by the hundreds in the bloody battle, and Columbus himself was wounded. He fought on furiously until his ship was rammed, then leaped into the water, grasping an oar that had floated free. Resting on the oar from time to time, he managed to swim the more than six miles to shore. Even this narrow escape did not make him lose his love of the sea, and he went on other voyages, going as far north as Ireland.

COLUMBUS PLANS HIS VOYAGE

Columbus now began to talk about his great dream. He could sail a ship straight west and reach the Orient with its riches of gold, gems, and spices. When friends asked how far he thought the voyage would be from Portugal to Japan he gave the distance at about three thousand nautical miles. This would have placed Japan in the approximate location of the Virgin Islands.

Old sailors laughed, and muttered that he was out of his mind. Undiscouraged, Columbus appealed for help to King John II of Portugal. The king's advisors on navigation called his plan nonsense, and the king himself was shocked by the demands Columbus made. If his voyage should prove successful, Columbus wanted noble rank, the title of admiral, a share of the profits, and governorship of any lands he discovered!

Columbus carried his dream to Spain and at first he did no better in the court of King Ferdinand and Queen Isabella. Spain was at war with the Moors and could spare no money for Columbus. And the Spanish experts laughed as loudly at his wild idea as had the Portuguese.

But Queen Isabella did not laugh. If necessary, she would pawn the crown jewels to fit out an expedition for Columbus. To keep her from taking this step, the royal treasurer somehow raised the money. In round figures, it came to $14,000.

AMERICA DISCOVERED

Sailing west, Columbus finds a new world. Even after four voyages he believes it is Asia, and the land is named for another navigator.

In the port of Palos before sunrise on August 3, 1492, three ships, carrying ninety men under Columbus's command, hoisted sail. As the wind caught the canvas, the *Santa Maria,* the *Niña,* and the *Pinta* moved toward the open sea. Many were the rewards the king and queen had promised the first man who sighted land, including the sum of 10,000 *maravedis,* an old Spanish coin of considerable value. Putting in at the Canary Islands, off the coast of West Africa, the ships were refitted. When they took to the sea again, the date was September 6, 1492.

Now, if the calculations of Columbus were correct, Japan was 2,400 nautical miles away. The world beyond the horizon was

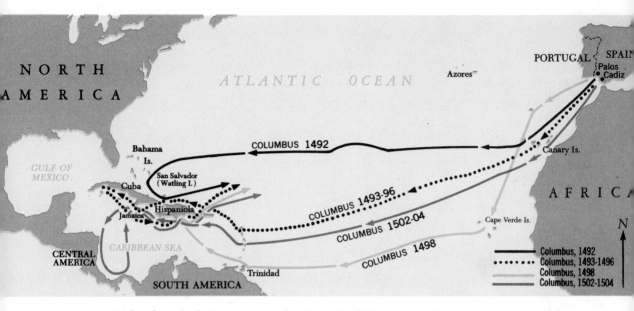

NORTH AMERICA

ATLANTIC OCEAN

Azores

PORTUGAL SPAIN

Palos
Cadiz

GULF OF MEXICO

Bahama Is.

COLUMBUS 1492

Canary Is.

San Salvador (Watling I.)

Cuba

AFRICA

Hispaniola

COLUMBUS 1493-96

Jamaica

COLUMBUS 1502-04

Cape Verde Is.

N

CENTRAL AMERICA

CARIBBEAN SEA

COLUMBUS 1498

——— Columbus, 1492
••••••• Columbus, 1493-1496
——— Columbus, 1498
——— Columbus, 1502-1504

Trinidad

SOUTH AMERICA

Columbus made four trips to the New World between 1492 and 1502. He explored the West Indies and touched the coasts of Central and South America, but never reached North America.

unknown. Who could say that the sea monsters of which sailors sometimes spoke—monsters that could swallow a ship in a gulp—did not exist here? For two weeks the three vessels plunged forward. The men on board, seeing nothing but sky and water, began to grumble among themselves. Pelicans flew over the ships, but a day passed, then another and another, and although other pelicans appeared, there was no sight of land. Masses of seaweed in the water aroused another fear. Suppose the weed should become so thick that the ships stuck in it? And then there was the wind that was blowing them away from Spain. How could they be sure that another wind would blow them home?

The grumbling grew worse. The crews met secretly, declaring that Columbus was risking their lives to carry out his own mad ambitions. Even though land had not been sighted, why should they not turn back? Would they not be honored for the fact that they had sailed farther west from Spain than any men who ever had gone to sea?

Some even plotted to heave Columbus overboard and claim he had fallen into the sea.

Late in September a cry rang out aboard the ships, "Land, land, sir!" The men murmured prayers of thanksgiving, but Columbus knew that by morning they would realize they had only seen some storm clouds that resembled an island. Despite the threats of his crew, Columbus kept his vessels plunging westward. So many false cries of land were raised that in early October Columbus issued a harsh order. Anyone who claimed to see land that was not reached within three days would forfeit the reward even if later he was the first to sight a shore.

THE FLEET NEARS LAND

On the afternoon of Thursday, October 11, there came a change. A green branch was sighted in the water, and then a green fish of the kind found near reefs. A stick, skillfully carved, was fished from the sea, and a sailor saw a thorn branch with red berries that seemed to be freshly cut. Even 15

Thirty-six days after leaving the Canaries, Columbus and his men were once more in harbor.

Columbus now believed that land was near, and to the other rewards for the first to sight it he added a velvet doublet.

About two hours before midnight, standing on the deck of the sterncastle, Columbus thought that he saw a light. He called on deck Pedro Gutiérrez, butler to the king, and Pedro, too, said that there had been a light. Then the *Pinta*, speediest of the three vessels, fired a signal. Land had been sighted by a sailor named Rodrigo de Triana.

Throughout that night the ships waited for daylight. The first rays of the rising sun on Friday, October 12, 1492, revealed the treelined coast of Watling Island in the Bahamas. Naked people could be seen along the water's edge, and Columbus boarded the little boat that would take him ashore.

With the royal banner of Spain and the cross of his faith, Columbus went ashore.

Proudly he carried the royal banner with its beautiful green cross that bore the letter F for Ferdinand on one arm and the letter Y for Ysabella (Isabella) on the other.

The sailors knelt in thanks to God. Some could not hold back their tears of joy and others kissed the ground. Columbus gave the island the name of San Salvador and claimed it for the king and queen. The In- dians watched the ceremony with gentle good manners. Columbus gave them little red caps and glass beads which they hung around their necks.

Columbus wrote in his journal that the Indians had "very handsome bodies and very good faces." Their hair, he said, was as coarse as a horse's tail, and they wore a braid in back that they never cut. Some 17

Columbus had his coat of arms made in 1502. The design at bottom left represents the islands that he had found.

A brisk trade developed between the sailors and the Indians, who came loaded down with skeins of spun cotton, parrots, and darts. Everything the Indians offered, Columbus said, was given with "as much love as if their hearts went with it." He could not watch these simple, generous people being cheated by his crew and issued stern orders against offering them in trade "bits of broken crockery" and other worthless items.

Still certain that Japan was near, Columbus sailed to the island Hispaniola (now Haiti and the Dominican Republic). Here he built a fort and left forty-four men while he hastened home with the news of his remarkable discoveries. He was received in triumph at the Spanish court. People stared at the rich and strange prizes from the new-found lands—the cotton, the samples of gold, the strange plants, birds, and animals, the Indians he had brought to be baptized. Plans were made for a second voyage.

Bad news awaited Columbus on his return to Hispaniola. His fort was burned and his colonists had disappeared. Building a second fort and founding the city of Isa-

painted their faces, some their whole bodies, some only their noses, using shades of black and white, red and blue. All seemed to have very broad foreheads, the result of their custom of flattening the skulls of infants by pressing them between boards. They were highly intelligent and could repeat words that they had heard only once.

Columbus marveled at the boats in which the Indians came to visit the ships. Built all in one piece from the trunks of trees, they sometimes carried as many as forty paddlers. They were "wonderfully made" and skimmed through the water with speed and grace.

This was the first map to bear the name America. Cut this way it fits over a ball to form a globe.

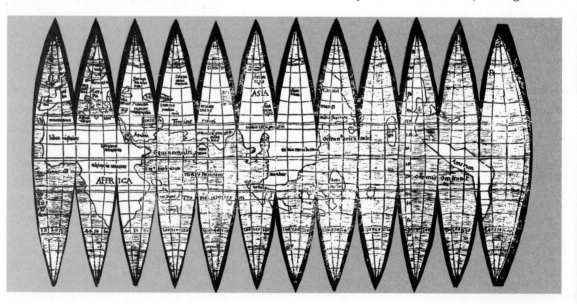

When he was safely back in Spain, Columbus told King Ferdinand and Queen Isabella of his discovery. They gave him permission to make another voyage.

bella, Columbus made a fresh start as a colonizer. But his love for the Indians was not shared by all. Wealth was what the followers of Columbus were seeking—in gold, in slaves. And Columbus was more a navigator and explorer than a governor. Always he wanted to continue sailing westward until he reached the treasures of the Far East.

In all, Columbus completed four voyages. He discovered the vast continent of South America and many important islands, among them Cuba and Jamaica.

When he died on May 20, 1506, Columbus still did not know that he had stumbled upon a new world.

But another Italian navigator of the day, Amerigo Vespucci, realized that these lands were not part of Asia. Between 1497 and 1504, he may have made as many as four voyages to the New World and claimed to be the first explorer to set foot upon the continent of South America. A map, published in 1507, gave the name of America to South America. Later geographers gave the name to both continents.

19

THE SEVEN CITIES OF GOLD

Three Spanish adventurers and a Moorish slave escape death and follow the trail of a legend.

On September 25, 1513, the Spanish explorer Balboa and his followers discovered the Pacific Ocean.

Six hundred years of war against the Moors had left Spain bankrupt. Some enormous stroke of good luck was needed to save the empire from ruin. The Spanish still believed the legend of a mysterious island in the ocean called Antillia to which, long centuries ago, seven religious men had sailed. Here, the priests had built the Seven Cities of Antillia, cities of such wealth that even the streets were paved with gold.

During the first thirty years of the Sixteenth Century, the quest for the Seven Cities led many fortune seekers to follow the sea lanes into the New World. Only seven years after Columbus had died, Vasco Núñez de Balboa led a ragged band across Panama and Europeans gazed for the first time upon the blue waters of the Pacific Ocean. By 1521 the brave and cruel Hernando Cortés had captured Mexico from the Aztec Indians, and in another year the ships of Ferdinand Magellan sailed the globe, proving that the world was round. Yet not all who left for the New World were so lucky. For years mystery surrounded the fate of the more than 250 men who sailed with Álvar Núñez Cabeza de Vaca in 1528.

A hurricane in the Gulf of Mexico wrecked this Spanish fleet off the Texas coast, and those who drowned were more fortunate than those who were eaten by cannibal Texas Indians. The wonder was that any survived. Yet Vaca waded from the stormy sea onto Galveston Island, where the natives made him a slave.

CABEZA DE VACA CROSSES TEXAS

Within a year Vaca escaped into the interior of Texas. Soon he became famous among the natives as a medicine man who achieved remarkable cures by using prayers and the sign of the cross. Five years after the shipwreck, traveling along the Colorado River near the Texas coast, Vaca came upon three other survivors. Dorantes and Cas-

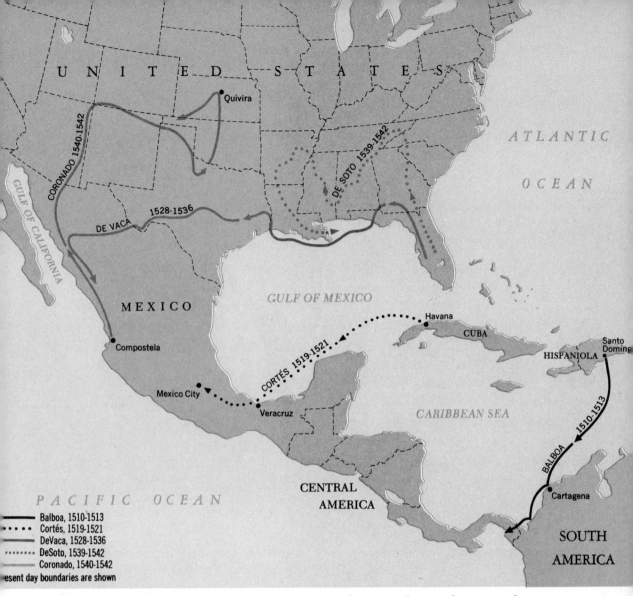

Early explorations in America. The boundaries shown are those of the present day.

tillo, like Vaca, were Spaniards. The other was Stephen, Dorantes' Moorish slave.

In the months that followed, Vaca and his party went up the Colorado River, journeyed west through the mesquite country, and in time crossed the Pecos River. Everywhere in western Texas crowds appeared. Simply to touch the garments of these castaways, the Indians believed, would heal their wounds and cure their illnesses. Stephen, the Moorish slave, became an idol, not only because he carried a gourd rattle that the Indians believed possessed mysterious powers, but also because he learned to speak their language. Gifts were show-

ered upon the travelers—beads, buffalo skins, pouches filled with pearls.

Some distance above present-day El Paso, Vaca and his friends crossed the Rio Grande. They saw Indians who lived in permanent homes and ate beans, squashes, and maize (corn). The first Europeans to visit New Mexico and Arizona, the Spaniards and their Moorish comrade heard tales of rich cities to the north where even the arrowheads sparkled like emeralds. Their eyes glittered as they remembered the old legend of Antillia. The Indians must be describing the famous Seven Cities of Gold —in a northern land called Cíbola.

Eight years had passed since Vaca's ship had been wrecked when one day a party of slave hunters, invading the coast of Texas, saw an almost unbelievable sight. Toward them traveled three Europeans and a Moor, accompanied by a band of 600 Indians who treated the four ragged castaways as gods. The slave hunters listened to the stories the party told and their eyes, too, glittered over those wonderful Seven Cities somewhere to the north.

THE SPANIARDS SEARCH FOR WEALTH

Fortune hunters discover a mighty river and other wonders of a strange continent, but fail to find gold.

During the eight years that Vaca and his companions had wandered across southwestern America, Spaniards under the mighty Pizarro had seized Peru from the Inca Indians. Yet even the stolen wealth of Peru, added to the captured riches of Mexico, was not enough to satisfy the greedy Spaniards. They listened eagerly to tales about the Seven Cities.

No one listened more closely than Hernando de Soto, who had fought with Pizarro in Peru. De Soto talked with a survivor of Vaca's party, and his heart beat faster. He wanted wealth and power. Like Cortés in Mexico and Pizarro in Peru, he would conquer and rule an empire of his own.

In the spring of 1539, de Soto reached Havana and collected nine ships and 620 men for his expedition to capture the Seven Cities. He set sail for Florida—Land of Flowers—discovered years before by Juan Ponce de León. Ponce de León had been searching for "Bimini," where, according to Indian legend, bathing in the waters would give a person eternal youth. In-

stead, he found the natives becoming more and more suspicious of Spaniards who carried the cross in one hand and the sword in the other. Ponce de León and his men had been driven back to their ships.

But in those days Spaniards believed that heaven intended them to do as they pleased in this land of heathen redskins. De Soto was no exception, and, late in the spring of 1539, he landed his expedition on the shore of Charlotte Bay on the west coast of Florida. He brought ashore his knights and soldiers in armor, more than 200 horses, and hundreds of hogs on the hoof. Two years of nightmare followed. Almost constantly at war with the Indians, he led his men through the wilderness of Florida and up into Alabama, Tennessee, and the Carolinas. They found hunger, sickness, and death rather than gold.

De Soto had enormous difficulty moving his troops and artillery.

In late April or May of 1541, de Soto stumbled upon a river—the mighty Mississippi—but it meant little to him. At least 200 of the knights and soldiers who had started with him now were dead, and those who survived wore raccoon and wildcat furs under their rusty armor.

The Spaniards had reached the Mississippi some thirty or thirty-five miles below the present city of Memphis, and at this point the treacherous old river was a mile wide. They hollowed out logs to make dugouts or canoes and on June 29, 1541, they landed on the soil of Arkansas near Sunflower Landing, south of Helena. "A man standing on the shore could not be told, whether he were a man or something else, from the other shore," wrote one of these first white voyagers on the Mississippi. "The stream was swift, and very deep. The

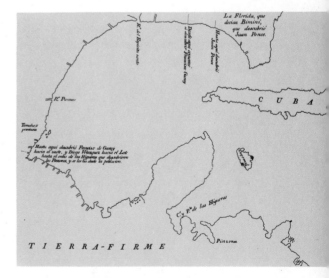

The Gulf of Mexico, sketched in 1520.

23

water, always flowing turbidly brought . . . from above many trees and much timber, driven onward by its force. There were many fish of several sorts, the greater part differing from those . . . of Spain."

Still determined to find wealth, de Soto and his tattered band explored the central part of Arkansas. They crossed the Arkansas River and discovered a "very warm and brackish lake" that must have been the now-famous Hot Springs. After two years the Spaniards had not changed their style of conquest. Indians were treated as slaves or fools, and usually as both. De Soto bragged that he was a god who possessed powers making him all-wise. He showed the red men a mirror he carried. In its glass, he declared, was revealed everything they did and thought. But the Indians, far from being fools, played their own game with de Soto. Always they spoke of places of great wealth somewhere in the distance, and by this trick rid themselves of the Spaniards, who pressed on in their search for fortune.

DE SOTO DIES

De Soto and his party wandered down the Ouachita River before camping for the winter. Pitifully weakened, they lived on a little corn, beans, pecans, and dried persimmons grudgingly supplied by neighboring Indians. Malaria broke out and one by one the Spaniards began to die. By May the eyes of de Soto burned with fever. Late that month the captain died and the new captain general of the expedition, Luys Moscoso de Alvarado, feared what the Indians might do when they discovered that the Spanish leader was not an immortal god.

To avoid trouble with the Indians, de Soto was buried secretly in the sands of the Mississippi.

The Zuñi Indians built settlements of sun-dried brick on the tops of high cliffs.

For three days de Soto's corpse was hidden. Then by night it was taken to the middle of the great river de Soto had discovered and buried in the sands of the Mississippi. The Indians, however, were instantly suspicious. They ordered two young Spaniards to be slain, for it was their custom, when any lord died, to kill some persons who should accompany and serve him on the way to the happy hunting grounds. Luckily, the Spaniards avoided this sacrifice by insisting de Soto was not dead but had merely returned to heaven, taking with him all the soldiers he required for that journey.

Although in later months the Spaniards under Moscoso pushed into Missouri, they never found the Seven Cities. Only 320 survivors—300 less than had started—accompanied Moscoso when in the fall of 1543 the expedition ended in Mexico.

CORONADO SEEKS GOLD

But another Spanish expedition already had discovered the Seven Cities of Cíbola. Francisco Vásquez de Coronado, governor of one of the northern districts of Mexico, also had listened eagerly to the tales Vaca's party brought back. In February, 1540, Coronado set forth with an expedition of 250 horsemen, seventy Spanish footmen, hundreds of friendly Indians, and herds of baggage animals and cattle.

Coronado's band was high-spirited and eager for adventure. Like most Spanish explorers of the time, these soldiers of fortune were young men. Many were still boys outgrowing their teens, and most of the others were in their early twenties. By July they reached the Zuñi River country, close to the present-day boundary between New Mexico and Arizona. A brisk fight one night in Bad Pass was sharp warning that the Spaniards were unwelcome visitors.

The Zuñi tribesmen who watched the approach of Coronado and his soldiers were a proud people. How long they had inhabited this desert country was a mystery. Some experts believe they already had lived in America for at least 10,000 years, and others think 15,000 years may be a more accurate guess. At least ten centuries before Coronado appeared they had built dwellings four and five stories high, containing as many as 1,200 rooms.

The Zuñi Indians, whom the Spaniards would call Pueblos—*pueblo* meaning *village* in Spanish—constructed their homes of desert earth and rock. These first apartment houses in America were set on high cliffs. As a further protection from enemies, there were neither doors nor windows on the first floor. The only entry was by ladders that could be quickly raised in case of attack. When the sun shone on the colored earth and rock of these cliff cities, they sparkled as though made of precious metals—and it was this that fooled Coronado's men.

25

Catching a glimpse of the Zuñi village of Hawikuh, they cried, *"Albricias! Albricias!"* or, "Reward me! Reward me!"

They were overjoyed. They had found Cíbola! But the Indians fought savagely to save their city. And when, after much bloodshed, the Zuñis finally were subdued, the Spaniards discovered that all they had conquered was a little pueblo of earth and rock. Indeed, there were Seven Cities of Cíbola—seven little pueblos like Hawikuh, all worthless to these treasure seekers.

CORONADO EXPLORES THE GRAND CANYON

Coronado quickly forgot the disappointment of Cíbola and led his expedition west-ward to the Rio Grande. His soldiers explored northeastern Arizona and the Grand Canyon of the Colorado River. Here the Indians streaked their faces with black soot and often wore masks of the same color. They were sun worshippers, and the Spaniards described them in these words:

"Some have their noses pierced, and from them hang pendants, while others wear shells. They also have their ears pierced with many holes, in which they place shells and beads. All of them, big and little, wear a multi-colored sash around the waist, and, tied in the middle, a round bundle of feathers hanging down like a tail. . . . They carry small blades of deer bones tied around one arm, with which they scrape off sweat, and

As the rays of the sun struck the distant pueblo, Coronado thought he had found the city of gold.

26

from the other reed canes are hung. They have also a kind of sack a span [nine inches] long tied to the left arm, using it as an arm-bag for the bow, and it is filled with seeds from which they make a sort of beverage. Their bodies are branded by fire. Their hair is banged in front, but in the back it hangs to the waist."

New stories reached Coronado of a place of untold wealth far to the northeast called Quivira. With spring he was off once more, crossing the plains of Texas and finding nothing. Still hopeful, he retraced his way and marched northward into central Kansas.

At times on the prairies Coronado seemed to be "swallowed up in the sea," for there was "not a stone, nor a bit of rising ground, nor a tree, nor a shrub, nor anything to go by." He passed vast herds of buffalo. The Texas Indians who guided the Spaniards lived on the raw flesh and blood of these animals. Except when they stopped to hunt buffalo, the Indians traveled swiftly behind the dogs they had trained as pack animals.

Reaching Quivira after a weary march of seventy-seven days, Coronado looked with scorn upon the houses of straw in which "barbarous" Wichita Indians lived. Like the Texans, the Wichitas were raw-meat eaters. Yet Coronado could not hide his delight in this Kansas country, calling it "the best I have ever seen for producing all the products of Spain, for besides the land itself being very flat and black and being well watered by the rivulets and springs and rivers, I found prunes like those of Spain and nuts and very good sweet grapes and mulberries."

Coronado's expedition was a failure, and in the spring of 1542 he returned to Mexico.

SPAIN CLAIMS THE NEW WORLD

Half a century had passed since Columbus had discovered the New World. Now two great continents—North America and South America—were claimed by Spain. Her navigators were familiar with the entire coast of the Gulf of Mexico and with the coast of the Atlantic at least as far as Newfoundland. De Soto had marched his knights in rusty armor to the banks of the Mississippi and Coronado had hunted buffalo on the prairies of Kansas. The habits of the Indians, as old if not older than the Spaniards themselves, were becoming common knowledge.

Spain never realized that the land and the people were the real wealth it sought. Other European nations would soon invade the New World and fight for an empire. What no one could guess was that, with time, they *all* would lose.

27

John Cabot, an Italian by birth, sailed the first English ship to explore the New World.

THE SEARCH FOR THE NORTHWEST PASSAGE

France becomes a rival to Spain and Portugal in the New World as her explorers try to find a waterway to the East.

During the 1490's, England's seaport of Bristol was crammed with sailors and merchants who lived by the sea. They were greatly excited by the news of Columbus's first voyage to the West Indies. Merchants who had grown wealthy on trade with the fisheries of Iceland became eager for even greater profits in the lands the Spaniards had discovered. The idea grew that perhaps there was a sea route—a northwest passage —around the newly discovered land blocking the way to the Orient. On a May day in 1497, the wharves of Bristol were thronged with well-wishers who cheered and waved as the first British vessel sailed westward in search of the riches of the East.

The name of this sturdy little ship was the *Matthew* and her crew numbered eighteen men. At the helm stood John Cabot, a native of Genoa and for many years a merchant in Venice. Little more is known about Cabot—or Giovanni Caboto, as he was called in Italy. All that can be said with certainty about his voyage is the fact that he claimed to have discovered in late June what he supposed was the Chinese coast "in the territory of the Grand Chan." In another month Cabot and his crew returned to Bristol, with wild tales of triumph, and in London high honors were heaped upon him. "He is called the Grand Admiral," reported an account written at the time. "He is dressed in silk, and the English run after him like madmen."

The best guess is that Cabot had landed somewhere on Cape Breton Island at the northern tip of Nova Scotia. On a second voyage the following year, Cabot evidently was lost at sea—at least no word was ever heard from him again. Later voyages were made by his son, Sebastian Cabot. Through the exploits of the Cabots, father and son, England could claim to have been the first European nation whose navigators had set foot on the continent of North America; Columbus had landed only in the West Indies.

JACQUES CARTIER SEEKS THE NORTHWEST PASSAGE

Spain and Portugal, with the approval of the Pope, divided the New World between them. They forbade other nations to invade their "sacred rights" as England had done through the voyages of the two Cabots. Then, in 1534, France became a new rival in the struggle for possession of the New World. On April 20, two French ships set sail from St. Malo in search of the Northwest Passage that the Cabots had failed to find. At the head of this expedition was another man of mystery, Jacques Cartier, who left no record of his youth beyond the fact that he was born at St. Malo in France.

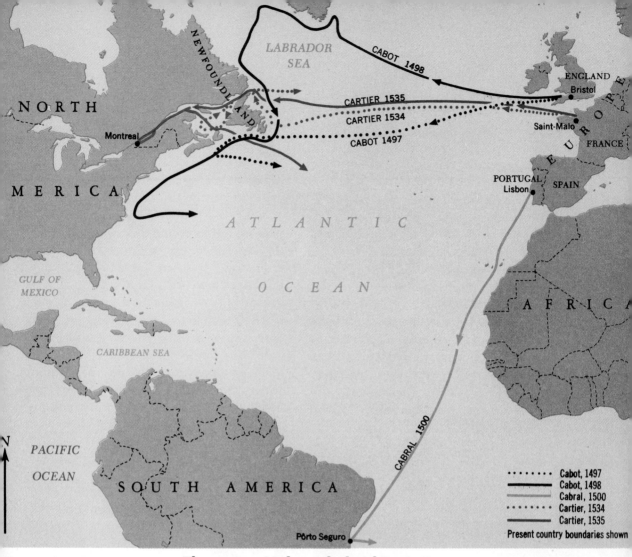

The voyages of Cabot, Cabral, and Cartier.

Cartier sighted Newfoundland on May 10 and planted the cross of France at Gaspé Bay. The following summer, Cartier returned to North America with a fleet of three ships. He heard of a great river and of a populous island town called Hochelaga, situated hundreds of miles upstream. Although Cartier was sure this river was not the passage he sought to the Orient, he decided to make the journey to Hochelaga.

For two weeks Cartier voyaged up the broad St. Lawrence River, finding a fine harbor at the site of the present city of Quebec. Here he anchored his three ships and continued the journey in small boats. Near where Montreal would one day rise, the Frenchmen landed in early October.

Cartier received a hearty welcome from the Indians. Men, women, and children brought food and danced joyfully.

Next day the Frenchmen marched to Hochelaga along a well-beaten road through a forest of oaks as fine as any in France. Acorns covered the ground. Then the Frenchmen came upon large, cultivated fields "full of grain" and soon were entering the gate of the fortified town of Hochelaga. Within the enclosure were about fifty houses, made of timber frames and covered with bark or strips of timber. Each dwelling had its large center room where the fire was built and the family lived.

The king of these people was named Agohanna, and he wore a red band of porcupine 29 quills around his head as a symbol of authority. But Agohanna was a sick old man who asked Cartier to examine his sore, weakened legs and arms. When Cartier began to stroke these withered limbs with his own strong hands, Agohanna removed the red band and placed it on Cartier's head.

The gesture was a sign to the people to bring forward all who were ill. The blind, the one-eyed, the lame approached, and others "so very old that the lids of their eyes hung down even upon their cheeks." They all begged Cartier to cure them.

For centuries the Indians of North America had heard a legend that told how one day palefaced men from across the sea would come as healers. The Spaniards had proved the legend wrong; they were conquerors, not healers. But Cartier was a different kind of man. He gathered the Indians around him, read to them from the Gospel of St. John, made the sign of the cross on the sick and the lame, and offered prayers for their salvation. An eyewitness wrote: "All these poor people kept a great silence and were marvelously good hearers, looking up to heaven and making the same ceremonies that they saw us make."

Afterward Cartier gave tin plates to the women, knives to the men, and hatchets to the chiefs. He threw small rings on the ground and watched the children scampering after them with happy shouts. Cartier knew only one moment of embarrassment, when the Indians heaped food before his party—all of it unsalted and not to French taste. But Cartier thanked the Indians, explaining that his party was not hungry. From the beginning, these Frenchmen knew how to behave in the wilderness.

Cartier comforted the ailing Agohanna and made friends with the Indians.

OLD POWERS SEEK NEW EMPIRES

England seeks a place in the New World, and the first settlements are set up in North America. The mystery of the lost colony.

As the years went by, Spain's conquests in the New World made her rich and powerful. She interfered in the affairs of Portugal, Italy, France, and the Netherlands. Even in England, now ruled by Queen Elizabeth I, Spanish spies were hard at work.

Queen Elizabeth was a woman with a quick mind and a strong will, and the spies had many things to report. In the late 1570's Martin Frobisher made three voyages to Labrador in a vain search for gold. Then, in 1577, Francis Drake set off in the *Golden Hind* on a three-year voyage around the world, and Spain realized that England intended to develop into a first-class sea power.

As early as 1542, Juan Rodríguez Cabrillo, a Portuguese navigator employed by Spain, had sailed into San Diego Bay. Cabrillo had explored a considerable length of the coast of present-day California. He had discovered Santa Monica Bay and the three islands of the Santa Barbara group before he died of an illness. Yet Cabrillo's crew brought back no proof of gold in these regions, and Spain was little interested in the lands north of Mexico.

Then troubling reports reached Spain. In 1579, Drake sailed his *Golden Hind* up

To the English, Francis Drake was a hero, and Queen Elizabeth made him a knight.

the west coast of South America and finally into San Francisco Bay. The Indians, bearing gifts of feathers and tobacco, greeted the English as gods. Drake called these native Californians a people of "free and loving nature, without guile and treachery," and gave them "necessary things to cover their nakedness." Drake refused the pleas of the Indians to "take their province and kingdom into his hand and become their king." Instead, he claimed California for England and gave to the land the name of New Albion. He nailed a brass plate to a post "together with her Highness' picture and arms, in a piece of sixpence current English money."

Seeking the outlet of the fabled Northwest Passage, Drake voyaged along the coast of Oregon and as far north as British Columbia. He began to doubt that such a passage existed—or, if it did, that it was navigable—and it seemed to him the land ran continually northwest, "as if it went directly to meet with Asia." Quite correctly, Drake guessed that the continents of Asia and North America must be very close together if they did not actually join.

Elizabeth greeted Drake warmly on his return to England. She stored away in the Tower of London most of the treasure, worth millions of dollars, that he had brought back with him—treasure he had taken in raids on the Spaniards.

SIR HUMPHREY GILBERT SAILS NORTH

Less successful were the voyages of Sir Humphrey Gilbert. The first, in 1578, had been a secret so well kept that neither the Spanish nor anybody else could learn much about it. The instructions the queen gave Gilbert were "to search, find out and view such remote, heathen and barbarous lands, countries and territories not actually possessed of any Christian people or prince." Sir Humphrey, failing on his first try, sailed again in 1583. If, as some believe, Gilbert actually intended to sail to Florida, he went the wrong way. He took possession of Newfoundland, but misfortune followed him like a school of sharks. On the voyage westward he lost his flagship and the stores for his proposed colony. On the voyage home he was drowned when the bark *Squirrel* went down.

Yet Sir Humphrey Gilbert's voyages were far from complete failures, for they kept alive England's interest in North America. The queen's advisors urged her to plant colonies in the New World. The Spanish and the French were already there, and the Dutch would surely be there, too, as soon as the wars in the Netherlands ended.

What could be gained from colonies in North America? In the northern parts of the continent, the queen's advisors answered, the winters were long and cold,

The voyages of Sir Francis Drake. Present-day boundaries and places are shown.

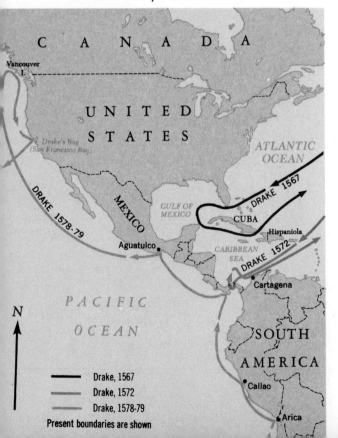

The storm that wrecked the French fleet helped the Spanish to keep control over Florida.

promising a good market for English woolen goods. Furs, which were a great rage in Paris, could be found in abundance in the New World. The fisheries of Newfoundland were another rich source of trade, and the French reported finding large deposits of red copper in the regions they had explored. There was still one more strong argument—Spain. How long should she be allowed to rule the roost, to stir up trouble all over Europe, and even send her spies into Elizabeth's own court?

This was dangerous talk, and Elizabeth kept it secret, for Spain was becoming increasingly warlike toward any nation that challenged her possessions in the New World. To guard against pirates roaming the Florida coast, Spain organized special fleets of armed vessels to escort her treasure ships on their homeward voyages. And Spanish tempers had boiled over in 1564 when the French, growing ever bolder in North America, landed in Florida and planted a colony at Fort Caroline on the St. Johns River.

Under the captain general of the Spanish treasure fleet, Don Pedro Menéndez de Avilés, an expedition was organized to rid Florida of these French invaders. In September, 1565, Menéndez brought his warships up the St. Johns River, but to his surprise the French fleet stood ready to give battle. A game of hide-and-seek between the two naval forces ended disastrously for the French when a storm shipwrecked their vessels. Menéndez at once made an attack on Fort Caroline, killing all the inhabitants of the colony except the women and children. He hunted the survivors of the wrecked fleet and cut them down with his sword.

FIRST PERMANENT WHITE SETTLEMENT IS BUILT

That same year, at St. Augustine, Florida, the Spanish founded the first permanent white settlement in this country, giving Menéndez a base from which to fight off invaders. Jesuit priests were sent to establish missions among the Indians and by 1571 they had settled as far north as the Potomac River, near the present city of Washington, D.C. Spanish vessels patrolled the coast of Florida and the Carolinas.

Queen Elizabeth knew these facts when she sent two barks to search for a site for a future colony along the southern part of the North American coast. On a bright April day in 1584 these ships left on the journey 33 that carried them to the low-lying coast that now belongs to North Carolina. Here, on an island to which the name of Roanoke would be given, the English believed that they had the ideal spot. They found the Indians on the mainland "most gentle, loving and faithful, void of all guile and treason."

SIR RICHARD GRENVILLE FOUNDS ROANOKE

The exciting reports these explorers brought home convinced Elizabeth, and a fleet commanded by Sir Richard Grenville was assembled to carry colonists to America. In June, 1585, Grenville landed his colonists on Roanoke Island and wrote a glowing account of what Elizabeth could expect from "her Majesty's new kingdom of Virginia." He had found the mainland "the goodliest soil under heaven." He described the abundance of "sweet trees" and of grapes, which were as fine as those found in France, Spain, and Italy. There were, in addition, "many

sorts of apothecary drugs" and among the many kinds of flax was one like silk. In this continent of "huge and unknown greatness" existed many people and towns in a climate so wholesome that he had not seen a single sick person. If Virginia were supplied with horses and cattle, and if Englishmen inhabited this country, no realm in Christendom would compare with it—or so, at least, Grenville reported.

Sir Richard left about a hundred colonists on Roanoke, promising to send a ship with supplies. Instead of cultivating the land, the settlers spent their time searching for gold and picking quarrels with the Indians—not the best way to start a new life in a new world. Then a hurricane struck the coast, making them wish they never had left England.

But relief was closer at hand than anyone dared hope. For weeks Sir Francis Drake had been raiding Spanish ships and towns in the West Indies. Then, unexpectedly, he appeared in the harbor of St. Augustine. He

The Spanish in St. Augustine fled in terror when Drake invaded and set fire to it.

34

burned that place to the ground while the Spaniards hid in the nearby swamps and swore savage oaths of revenge on these English vandals. Drake sailed on to Roanoke, where he found the colonists still trembling from their experience with the hurricane. He agreed to take them all home.

In a short time the promised supply ship arrived at Roanoke, but when no colonists were found, it turned back to England. Grenville also appeared with three ships and spent days sailing along the coast trying to learn what had happened to his colony. Unwilling to lose possession of the country, Grenville left fifteen men with provisions for two years to hold the fort on Roanoke.

In April of 1587 still another expedition of colonists was sent under the command of John White. He reached Roanoke in June, but found the fort demolished. Of the fifteen men Grenville had left, there was only a single skeleton!

White rebuilt the fort, erected a few houses, and named his new settlement "the

Sir Francis Drake

Citie of Raleigh in Virginia." That August, his granddaughter, Virginia Dare, became the first child of English parents born in North America. White returned to England, promising a speedy return.

He intended to keep his word, but England was engaged in a long and exhausting war with Spain. In 1588 every good ship England could find was needed to fight off the threatened invasion of the island by the Spanish Armada of 130 vessels, 2,500 guns, and 30,000 men. Storms helped a plucky English fleet to drive off the Armada. "God blew and they were scattered," the English said afterward—and, surely, it must have seemed no less than a miracle.

THE LOST COLONY OF ROANOKE

John White, after four years, at last could carry his promised supplies to Roanoke. A shock—and a mystery—awaited him. Not a single colonist remained. He found chests, books torn from their covers, and armor "almost eaten through with rust." The word "CROATOAN" was carved on one tree and the letters "CRO" on another.

What did it mean? Had the colonists been murdered by Spaniards? Had they been killed by Indians—or, equally possible, had they wandered off to live with the Indians? No one has ever answered these questions. 35

Planting the Tree of Liberty

After many hardships, the English establish a colony at Jamestown and make a start at governing themselves.

In 1603, with the death of Queen Elizabeth, James I became the ruler of England. As he journeyed from his home in Scotland to his court in London, he saw few things to make him cheerful. England had paid dearly for her long years of war with Spain. Beggars filled the streets of the cities and vagabonds roamed country roads. Prices were high and wages were low. Many people awoke each morning without work or hope, and far too often they went to bed hungry. A new life in the New World became their only chance of escaping from these miseries. England decided to make a success of building colonies in North America.

The voyages of Gilbert to Newfoundland and Grenville to Roanoke had taught the English a hard lesson. Starting a new nation in a wilderness was too large an undertaking for one man to run. Now trading companies were organized, with noblemen, merchants, and private citizens investing in them for a share of the profits. A trading company elected its own officers, made its own by-laws, and even coined its own money. It could arm its own soldiers to defend its settlements.

Under James I, two principal companies were chartered to establish colonies in North America, and to each the king granted a tract of land a hundred miles in width and a hundred miles in depth. By December, 1606, the Virginia Company of London was ready to start its colony. When the three ships—the *Susan Comfort,* the *Godspeed,* and the *Discovery*—sailed from Blackwell dock that chilly day, their passengers included two goldsmiths, two refiners, and a jeweler, for the investors still believed that Virginia possessed great quantities of precious ores. They believed, too, that somewhere in the New World was a river that would lead to the South Sea and the riches of the Orient.

The ships carried a strange mixture of people. Among them was Captain John Smith, who told unbelievable tales of fighting in the Netherlands, Hungary, and Turkey. He told of his capture by the Turks, of

his hardships as a slave in Constantinople, and of his escape across the desert. Another voyager was Captain Bartholomew Gosnold, who had sailed to America in 1602 and landed on the Elizabeth Islands off that strip of Massachusetts coast he named Cape Cod. A third was Edward Brookes, gentleman, who died on the way because—or so it was reported—his "fat melted within him." A fourth was John Layden, carpenter, who would claim a place in history by marrying a maidservant in the first English marriage ceremony on the soil of Virginia.

So they came together—nobleman and peasant, soldier of fortune and craftsman— in all, 144 settlers. They set sail in good spirits, believing that the Indians of Virginia devoted their holidays to gathering diamonds and rubies along the seashore.

Many storms tossed their ships as they sailed to Virginia, but at four o'clock in the morning on April 26, 1607 they sighted the promised land. When they went ashore next day, they were delighted with the tall trees, fair meadows, and streams of sparkling fresh water. But that afternoon, as the explorers

The Virginia colonists feasted with the Indians in celebration of the peace they had made.

were returning to their boats, the Indians attacked—"creeping upon all fours from the hills, like bears, with their bows in their mouths."

Somehow the colonists made peace with the Indians, and they held a great feast. Their bodies smeared with red and black clay, the Indians staged a dance of welcome. One Indian stood in the center of the group, singing and beating one hand against another. The others danced around him, "shouting, howling, and stamping against the ground." They twisted and turned, screwed up their faces, and made a noise "like so many wolves or devils."

Wonderful discoveries filled each day— on the beaches where the mussels and oysters lay "as thick as stones," in the meadows where the strawberries were "four times bigger than ours in England." One day the English saw a strange sight: an Indian boy of about ten years of age with "a head of a perfect yellow and a reasonable white skin." Could he have been a descendant of one of the survivors of the Lost Colony of Roanoke?

By mid-May the colonists agreed upon a site for their settlement, calling the place Jamestown in honor of the king. With good sense, they started at once to build a fort. The beauty of Virginia was all about them. The woods were filled with beech, oak, cedar, cypress, walnut, and sassafras trees. Flowers spread blankets of bright color on the hillsides. Strawberries, mulberries, raspberries, and other fruits grew in abundance, and the rivers teemed with fish. Squirrels raced through the trees and the birds flashed

The Jamestown settlers put up a wall of heavy logs to protect themselves from Indian attacks.

wings of crimson, blue, olive, and white. Nests of turkey eggs seemed to be everywhere and the settlers also found deer, bears, foxes, otters, beavers, muskrats, "and wild beasts unknown."

A FORT IS COMPLETED AT JAMESTOWN

The fort was completed in a month and two days. By late June the ships were ready to return to London for supplies. What followed for the 104 settlers who remained at Jamestown was a nightmare.

Close to the settlement were stagnant swamps which bred mosquitoes and disease during the humid summer months. Storms frequently raised the tides in the river so that its salty water overflowed, spoiling the springs that supplied drinking water. At such times the fish, which had been a main source of food, moved upstream to quieter waters. Canoes were smashed by high tides. Winds tore fishing nets to shreds.

Worn out from their long journey and the work of building a settlement, the colonists no longer had the strength to fight off this unexpected combination of disasters. Within ten days after the ships had sailed back to London, the settlers came down with sicknesses that left them almost too weak to walk or stand. Almost every day

Captain John Smith

someone complained of severe stomach cramps or burning fever. Many died. Quarrels broke out among the leaders of the colony. At the end of five months not five men could be found capable of standing guard at the fort.

But then a miracle occurred. The Indians appeared with bread, corn, fish, and meat to save the starving settlement. Cooler weather dried up the disease-infested swamps. And, just as important, Captain John Smith became the real leader of the colony.

Smith may have told tall tales. He told of his adventures as a soldier of fortune in many parts of the world, but no one could deny that he saved the colony at Jamestown. Perhaps another tall tale was the story of his capture by the Indians and his escape from death when the beautiful princess, Pocahontas, threw her body upon his own to save him from the executioner. But if Smith's stories were astonishing, so also were his achievements. By April, 1609, the colony had begun to prosper. A glassworks produced the first manufacturers in North America. A well gave "excellent sweet water," and twenty houses and a church had been built. A blockhouse outside the fort guarded the settlement from surprise attack.

Other ships coming from London during this time increased the population of Jamestown to almost 500. Then John Smith returned to England. Within weeks the colony fell apart.

"THE STARVING TIME"

The dreadful winter of 1609-10—"the starving time"—followed. For each settler who survived at Jamestown, nine others died. The people ate dogs and cats, rats and mice, and hunted in the woods "to feed upon serpents and snakes." Here they were often stalked and killed by hostile Indians. Other settlers fished the rivers, eating anything drawn up in the nets—including boots or "any other leather." In spring the long

The Indian princess Pocahontas saved John Smith's life—at least that was the tale he told.

In 1614, Pocahontas married John Rolfe, one of the Jamestown colonists.

overdue supply ships, which had been blown off course and partly wrecked in Bermuda, finally reached the settlement. The survivors begged to be taken back to England. They were sailing down the James River, homeward bound, when at Hog Island they sighted another fleet bringing still more supplies to the colony.

Now the weary settlers faced a decision. Should they continue to England or turn back to Jamestown? At last, they agreed to try just once more.

For a colony to succeed in the wilderness, it had to produce some article of trade that the world wanted. So far, Jamestown had no such product. Glassmaking, the growing of silkworms, the cutting of timber, the manufacture of soap from ashes, the shipment of sassafras for medicinal purposes—all had failed to support the colony. But by this time a very remarkable man had reached Jamestown.

His name was John Rolfe. His baby had died after he was shipwrecked in Bermuda and his wife died shortly after he came to Jamestown. There seemed little reason for his staying at all. But John Rolfe would make history twice in America.

On a warm April day in 1614, Rolfe, an English gentleman, and Pocahontas, a "savage" princess, were married in the church at Jamestown. This was the same Pocahontas who was said to have saved the life of John Smith.

41

From winning the heart of a princess, Rolfe turned to changing the mind of a king. James I liked everything just as it always had been—from old shoes to old ideas. In particular, he stormed against the "filthy novelty" of using tobacco, a fad that was sweeping England. Smoking, James declared in a pamphlet he wrote, was "loathsome to the eye, hateful to the nose, harmful to the brain, and dangerous to the lungs." He told of one poor fellow—a user of tobacco—whose stomach at his death contained a bushel of soot.

Yet, while the king raged against tobacco, John Rolfe was carrying on an experiment that would save the king's settlement at Jamestown. The tobacco grown by the Indians in Virginia was strong and bitter, but Rolfe had brought to the colony seeds of the sweeter varieties of tobacco grown in the Caribbean Islands and South America. These varieties flourished in the soil of Virginia. The demand in Europe for this sweeter tobacco became so great that even the streets between the houses in Jamestown were plowed to grow the "weed."

Within a half-dozen years James I saw the "filthy novelty" he hated carry his colony at Jamestown from failure to success.

In the year 1619 three events occurred that changed the future of Virginia colony. In May and June a new kind of shipment arrived from England: a cargo of young women to marry the men who were carving an empire in the wilderness. Also during that spring, a Dutch ship appeared. It was badly in need of provisions, but all the captain could offer in trade were some twenty Negro captives. Thus, without plan, the first slaves were made part of the life of Virginia.

SELF-GOVERNMENT BEGINS IN AMERICA

By far the most important event took place on July 30. In the choir of the church at Jamestown, representatives from all the little settlements that now existed along the James River met in the first legislative assembly in America. One delegate who was not properly entitled to a seat in the as-

By importing new varieties of tobacco from the Caribbean and South America, John Rolfe was able to grow a milder and more mellow leaf than that which grew wild in Virginia.

sembly was rejected, and so upon a principle of fair representation, self-government started in America. Among the first offenders called before the lawmakers was one accused of using force to make the Indians trade with him. "Such outrages as this might breed danger and loss of life to others in the colony," read the complaint, stating clearly the purpose of self-government.

Laws reveal many things about people: what they want from life, how they live, even how they misbehave. This was true of

The men of Jamestown rejoiced in 1619 when a ship arrived bringing them brides from England.

the laws of those pioneer legislators who planted the seeds of liberty at Jamestown. Among their first acts they urged the adoption of a sensible method of collecting rents, petitioned England for the establishment of a college in the colony, and fixed the price for selling tobacco. Other laws dealt with personal behavior, and one decree ordered "that no injury or oppression be wrought by the English against the Indian whereby the present peace might be disturbed and ancient quarrels might be revived."

Other decrees called for severe punishments for idleness, gambling, drunkenness, the wearing of fancy clothes, and failure to observe religious customs. Another set of laws provided for the money to run the colony through the planting of corn, mulberry trees, silk flax, aniseed, and vineyards, and required the planters of Virginia to air their tobacco thoroughly before storage.

DEALINGS WITH THE INDIANS ARE CONTROLLED

Relations with the Indians were strictly regulated, for, declared the legislators, "they are a most treacherous people and quickly gone when they have done a villainy." So it became unlawful to sell or give an Indian an "English dog of quality," to supply him with arms or gunpowder, or to travel more than twenty miles from a settlement without the governor's permission. Finally a letter was sent to England, urging approval of all these laws.

Only a dozen years after the first colonists had knocked together a fort at Jamestown, only nine years after Lord Delaware had persuaded the miserable survivors of "the starving time" to turn back from Hog Island, two triumphs had been achieved. England had planted a permanent settlement in North America. And the colonists had planted, whether England liked it or not, a tree of liberty.

A BIRD FROM HEAVEN

The Dutch join the struggle for possession of the new land, and Hudson finds Indians, bays, and rivers.

Sooner or later, every explorer of the New World met native Americans. The Europeans, believing at first that they had reached India, called these natives Indians.

How the Indians first reached North America, no one can say for certain. The best theory is that a strip of land once linked Asia to Alaska, and the people journeyed by that route as long ago as the last Ice Age. When you look today at the Indian face on the buffalo nickel, you see features identical to those of people living in southwestern Tibet, a fact that perhaps suggests one link between past and present.

All that we can say with assurance is that the first migrations of Indians to our continent occurred tens of thousands of years ago. In time these wanderers from Asia spread across the land, following rivers, valleys, and mountain passes, until they occupied all regions of the continent. They broke into tribes, each group going its own way, until by the time of Columbus more than 400 such tribes existed. Each lived by the nature of the land where it settled—as farmers or hunters or fishermen. Some tribes did not advance much beyond the primitive life of the ancient Stone Age, while others developed highly organized societies.

Tribes had their own habits and customs, but other traits, such as a love of children, they shared in common. And they seemed to share also a kindness toward the white man when he first came to America. Was not this a trait that Columbus reported among the Indians of the West Indies, and Drake noted among the Indians in California, and Cartier found among the Indians in Canada? Grenville, in his first visit to Roanoke, was delighted with the gentleness of the natives of that island, and it was the generosity of the Indians that saved the settlers of Jamestown from starvation during their first wretched summer. With time, however, the white man's actions brought a change in this relationship.

THE PEACEFUL HUDSON VALLEY

In the valley of the Hudson River in 1609, no white man had yet appeared to meet the copper-skinned people who lived there. Giovanni da Verrazano, who explored the coast of North America under the flag of France, may have glimpsed the Hudson in 1524. If so, his visit may well have been the basis for an Indian legend about a bird that descended from heaven and then flew away—a bird so large that it carried men on its back. By 1609, however, almost a century had passed and no other

Tibetan (right) resembles the American Indian.

bird from heaven had been seen by the Indians who lived content beside "the stream that flows both ways."

The days of the Indians followed a pattern. Thus, there came for every Indian mother in the valley a day when she went

Indian life along the Hudson Valley was simple but happy before the white men came.

off by herself into the woods. Here, alone, whether the season was sweltering summer or snowy winter, she gave birth to her child. In time, she returned home, carrying her new baby with pride, for a joyous welcome awaited her. Every Indian loved a baby, for it was well known among these valley people that if an infant sensed he was unwanted, he would vanish into the Land of Lost Souls. And there was another danger. A baby that wasn't loved and watched could be carried off by an evil spirit. To safeguard the child from such deviltry, his ankles and wrists were tied to the ground for a time with cornhusks.

INDIAN LIFE IN THE HUDSON VALLEY

For all youngsters in the valley, life for the first ten years was a carefree time of learning the customs and lore of his people. He was taught the habits of the animals and how to hunt them. He was shown the great whales in the bay where the river emptied, and where the fish his family ate could be caught. The forest became both friend and foe, for bad spirits as well as good spirits lived here, and he learned to know where to expect each. He was taught which herbs and roots were good for food and medicine, and how to plant corn and make it grow. He watched his mother make the shoes he wore from cornhusks, and he saw her sew deerskin, elk hide, and beaver pelts to make the garments that kept him warm in winter.

Like all people in the valley, he admired the older, prosperous men of the tribe who strutted around in their splendid coats of turkey feathers. His sister prettied herself by painting blue and white rings around her eyes, weaving bands of snakeskin to go around her braided hair, and adorning her arms and neck with copper bracelets.

Wide-eyed, he saw a war party going off in their long canoes. Bonnets of eagle feathers encircled their heads, huge bear claws hung at their necks, and their faces were streaked with every color of the rainbow. He remembered how he had been taught to use a tomahawk, a hunting knife, and a bow and arrow, and he dreamed of the day when he too could go off on such a raid.

Now, with the women, the old men, the other children, he could only wait until shouts announced the party's return. He would dash to the river's edge, counting the scalps on the long poles the warriors held aloft and the captives that had been taken. Sometimes he journeyed with his people to

Canoe Place, which was neutral ground for meetings with the Indians from Rockaway, from Canarsie, and from across the bay in the country that one day would be called New Jersey. These were exciting times— for trading pelts and stories.

The Iroquois lived in "long houses" made of wood frames covered with bark. In summer, the women took care of the fields while the men hunted and fished. In winter, the men went out when they could, but mostly they lived indoors using up the supplies of food they had dried and stored away during the warm summer months.

Seeking a northwest passage, Hudson sailed up the river that was later to be named for him.

Then suddenly, in 1609, came the greatest wonder of a lifetime for all the people of the valley. There, coasting up their river, was a bird from heaven, its white wings spread to the wind and men walking upon its back! The Indians stared from their hiding places. The name on the prow of the ship was *Half Moon.*

THE DUTCH ARRIVE IN THE NEW WORLD

The *Half Moon's* arrival meant that still another nation—the Netherlands—was entering the struggle for possession of the New World. The *Half Moon* belonged to the Dutch East India Company. Its crew was part Dutch, part English, which suggests why more than once near mutiny had endangered its voyage to America. The leader of the expedition, Henry Hudson, already was famous in England as a navigator and an explorer. Others had sailed to the north*west* from Europe, looking for a passage to the Orient. Hudson, in two previous voyages for a British trading company, had sailed north*east,* seeking a passage through the ice barrier by way of the North Pole. Hudson's British backers were satisfied to take their profits from the whale fisheries he enabled them to establish at Spitsbergen, an island on the edge of the Arctic Ocean. If Hudson wanted to go on exploring for a northeast passage, he would have to find support elsewhere.

Hudson did—in Amsterdam. The little *Half Moon,* carrying its mixed crew of not more than twenty men, left Holland on April 4, 1609. A month later it rounded the Cape of Norway and Hudson came to a sea full of floating ice. In the bitter cold the crew fell into a quarrelsome mood, and Hudson at last agreed to reverse his course

49

and sail to the northwest. On May 14, the *Half Moon* came about, shaping her course toward the setting sun.

Hudson's hope of new discoveries was based in part on a letter he had recently received from his old friend in Virginia, Captain John Smith. Somewhere in the unexplored regions north of the colony at Jamestown, Hudson reasoned, could be an inland passage to the Orient. On the second of July, the *Half Moon* was off the Grand Banks of Newfoundland with foremast gone and sails torn. Proof that the French already had established themselves in the New World was the sight of a fleet of their ships fishing these waters, but Hudson "spoke with none of them." Mid-July brought him to the coast of Maine and safe harbor in what was probably Penobscot Bay. His crew remained troublesome, and when friendly Indians approached the *Half Moon* in two boats, they were savagely attacked for no reason.

Hudson did not hide his anger. He ordered the *Half Moon* once more to sea, and did not touch shore again until August 3, when his men brought back roses and sweet grapes. Hudson sailed on, believing he had reached the Cape Cod that Bartholomew Gosnold had named seven years before. When he discovered instead that he had entered the James River in Virginia, he was tempted to land and seek out his old friend, John Smith. Had he done so, he would have found that Smith was in England and the inhabitants of Jamestown were dying of dysentery and famine.

Beating north again, the *Half Moon* now embarked on a series of discoveries. Late August found Hudson and his crew rounding the lower capes and entering the body of water we now call Delaware Bay. Shoals of hidden sand scraping the bottom of the *Half Moon* discouraged Hudson from believing that this was the passage he sought to the Orient. Through early September he

The routes followed by Henry Hudson in his explorations aboard the Half Moon. *Present-day boundaries and places are shown.*

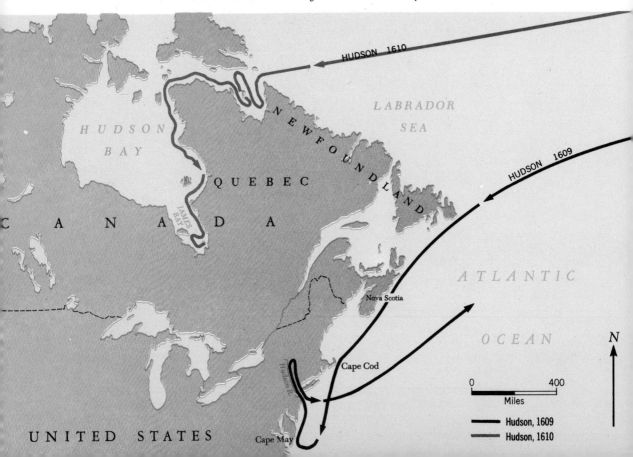

Cast adrift by his crew, Henry Hudson died in the great bay that bears his name.

coasted along New Jersey, seeking shelter from seasonal storms at Sandy Hook. He came at last to the bay that carried him into the river now bearing his name. The *Half Moon* sailed as far up river as what is now Albany before Hudson once more decided he had not yet discovered his northwest passage.

To the staring Indians the little vessel might have seemed like the bird of heaven, but she was more a creature of the devil. Hudson knew that his men were close to mutiny. He headed straight for Ireland before winter closed in around him.

Trouble filled the last years of Hudson's life. First there was resentment in England over the fact that he had sold his services to Holland and carried the Dutch into the New World. The following year, he sailed once more in search of the Northwest Passage, this time for a British company. In the midsummer of 1611, a faithless crew turned on Hudson, forcing him, his son, and several sick sailors to board a frail boat. The party was set adrift. Somewhere in the icy wastes of Hudson Bay, which he discovered, is "his tomb and his monument."

Yet the Dutch did not forget the New World, and soon other birds from heaven were winging their way across the Atlantic. Early in 1614, after a stormy voyage, Captain Adriaen Block reached New York Bay. There his ship burst into flames, and he and his crew passed a peaceful winter living among the Indians while they built a new ship to carry them home. This vessel they named *Onrust,* which in Dutch means "Restless." The name well expressed the spirit of the Hollanders, who in the years to come would sail the Atlantic in increasing numbers and string their trading posts all along the Hudson Valley.

CHAMPLAIN BLUNDERS BADLY

By aiding the Algonquin Indians, he earns the hatred of the powerful Iroquois, and France is the loser.

France made not only a late but an unlucky start in the New World. Her banner was carried by Samuel de Champlain, a capable man who was the son of a sea captain. Champlain had grown up along the coast of France knowing how to reef a sail and find his way by the stars. His first voyage to the North American continent was made in 1603. He explored the St. Lawrence River as far as the rapids above Montreal, and quickly became a warm friend of the Indians. The following year he explored the North American coast as far south as Cape Cod, and during the summer of 1608 he founded at Quebec the first white settlement in Canada.

But Champlain soon began to meddle in wilderness warfare. The spring of 1609 found the Algonquins and Hurons taking to the warpath against the Iroquois. Champlain chose to join the Algonquins and Hurons. He crossed the lake that would be named after him, and near present-day Ticonderoga pitched into a battle with the Iroquois. Champlain's weapon—an old matchlock gun called an arquebus—could be loaded with four bullets. His first volley, Champlain wrote, killed two Indians and wounded a third. Then a companion fired his arquebus and the battle was over. The astounded Indians "lost courage and took to flight."

Champlain had blundered badly, for the proud and powerful Iroquois remembered him with hatred for a century. They turned first to the Dutch and then to the English for allies. They were determined that the French would never gain a foothold in the land of the Iroquois.

Until the Seventeenth Century, the search for wealth and power had driven the Spanish and the English, the French and the Dutch to sail their little ships across the stormy Atlantic. For the most part these adventurers from Europe brought to the New World old European habits and customs and ideas—and old European jealousies that would in time produce a series of bloody wars. But soon a different kind of colonist would be making the long voyage to America.

BELIEVERS IN RELIGIOUS FREEDOM

English "Separatists" settle in Holland, but soon move to the New World to be able to worship God according to their beliefs.

In 1607 a violent quarrel broke out between hardheaded King James I and a little group of equally hardheaded English men and women. Anyone who knew James I quickly realized that he could only be happy when having his own way. As king, James I believed that he understood better than any of his subjects what was good for England. Even how the people should worship God, the king insisted, was a matter that he and his bishops alone could decide.

A stubborn group of Christians, called Separatists, challenged the right of the king to tell them how to manage their religious affairs. They said that no one should dictate who should preach to them, or in what manner, or in what company of fellow worshipers. As everyone expected, James I was displeased. The Separatists felt they must either carry on their religion as the king wished, or leave England.

Frightened by Champlain's gunfire, the Indians fled, leaving two of their number dead.

They chose to leave England, and during 1607-08 they went to Holland. For ten long years, as pilgrims in a strange land, they struggled to make a success of life among the Dutch in the city of Leyden. Farmers by training, they were forced to work hard at such city jobs as they could find. This sacrifice they bore cheerfully as long as they could worship God as they pleased. Yet as the Separatists grew older they began to wonder if they had any real future in Holland. Would not their religion disappear as, one by one, they went to their graves? Already their children were copying the ways of the easygoing Dutch. Who would keep them true to the Separatist faith?

Only a few at first suggested going to America and building a settlement in the wilderness where they could bring up their children as they wished. Others argued that the dangers in the New World were too great. But those who held out for making a new start in America spoke up forcefully. Why should they not run these risks? Were they afraid to trust in God to protect them?

In 1617 the Separatists at last decided to establish their own state in the New World. Three years later they finally were able to return to England to begin their voyage. Here they were joined by a "very mixed lot" of other voyagers who were more interested in seeking a fortune than religious

Trusting in God to protect them, the Pilgrims began their trip to the New World.

freedom. Right at the start one of the two boats they planned to use for the voyage began to leak so badly it had to be left behind. About one hundred in number, they crowded aboard a tiny ship called the *Mayflower,* and with tears and prayers and fearful hearts set sail for America on September 6, 1620. Those who were seeking their own religious state in America became known in history as the Pilgrims.

Fair winds at first carried the *Mayflower* across the sea toward her destination in northern Virginia. Then the weather turned. Fierce storms tossed the ship like a cork on the great rolling waves. Blustering winds tore sails to ribbons. Under the blows from the crashing sea, leaks appeared everywhere and one of the main beams cracked and sagged. The Pilgrims put their trust in God, propped up the sagging beam, patched the leaks, and sailed on. They lacked the lemons that would have given them vitamin C, and so they came down with a weakening sickness called scurvy. Yet only one of them died at sea.

That fact seemed a miracle, one of the three miracles by which the Pilgrims reckoned that God *did* bless and guide them. Another such sign was the case of a "proud and very profane" young sailor who cursed the Pilgrims in their misery and told them at least once a day that he hoped to throw

In 1620 they boarded the Mayflower *and left England to set up new homes in America.*

The Pilgrims looked on the rescue of a man who had fallen overboard as a sign of God's favor.

half of them overboard before the voyage ended. Instead, it was he who was taken ill, died in great agony, and was thrown overboard. A third sign was the fate of young John Howland, who was swept into the sea by a brutal wave. Howland grabbed a line and hung on until he could be fished back on deck with a boat hook.

After sixty-five troubled days they sighted land—not the coast of Virginia for which they had set sail, but the far-off shore of Cape Cod. They tried for half a day to sail southward, but shoals and roaring breakers drove them back to safe harbor off the coast of Massachusetts. They now faced a bewildering situation, for they had permission 57 to settle in Virginia, not in New England.

As the *Mayflower* rode at anchor, grumblings of mutiny were heard. Some of the passengers, more concerned with finding wealth than religious freedom, threatened to strike off on their own for Virginia. Others spoke up more calmly. They said they must stick together and draw up an agreement on the laws by which they would live until they could get permission from England to settle in this new country.

THE MAYFLOWER COMPACT

The document they wrote we now call the Mayflower Compact. Every male passenger signed it, pledging his honor to work with the others in passing and obeying such laws "as shall be thought most meet [fit] and convenient for the general good of the colony." Just as the settlers at Jamestown had planted a seed of liberty when they held their first legislative assembly in 1619, so did the Pilgrims plant a seed of democracy when they signed the Mayflower Compact on November 11, 1620.

For several weeks the Pilgrims searched the sandy New England coast for a suitable harbor and site of settlement. In late December they decided upon a place they called Plymouth, after the city in England where they had boarded the *Mayflower*. On Christmas day they started building their first common house, but in mid-January fire destroyed its thatched roof. This was only one of their many misfortunes.

A good part of their difficulty was the result of their own lack of planning. They had brought neither horses nor cattle, plows nor carts. Even their hooks and nets were too large for the fish that filled the waters all around them. Scurvy, influenza, and pneumonia made the winter months a time of horror. Sometimes two or three men

died in a single day, until by spring only half the colony survived. Not more than six or seven of those who lived could be described as being in good health.

One day the Indian chief Massasoit arrived at the settlement with sixty warriors. They could have easily wiped out all the Pilgrims, but they had come to offer their friendship and help. Among them was a remarkable Indian named Squanto, who had been captured by an earlier party of explorers and sold into slavery in Spain. He had escaped to England where he learned to speak the English language. To the Pilgrims he was like a messenger from heaven. Squanto taught the settlers how to plant

By the signing of the Mayflower Compact, the new settlers took a big step toward democracy.

corn and make it grow. He showed them how to build fish traps and stalk the game in the woods. He taught them how to catch and skin beavers, giving them a source of trade on which the colony at Plymouth would depend for many years.

All through the summer of 1621, with Squanto's help, the Pilgrims worked hard to raise corn. That fall they decided to hold a harvest festival. New England's first Thanksgiving lasted three days, and Indians and settlers alike enjoyed a gay time.

William Bradford became governor of the colony at Plymouth in 1621, and he was re-elected to that same position thirty times.

*Thanksgiving Day was celebrated for the first time in 1621
in Plymouth, Massachusetts by both settlers and Indians.
In addition to the other food, four wild turkeys were served.*

The sober black and gray clothes that the Pilgrims wore on the Sabbath were put aside for the garments of bright green and brown that they liked so much. Indians and settlers played games. They filled their bellies, too—on venison, roast duck, shellfish, corn bread, wild fruits, and berries. They drank the wine they had made from wild grapes.

But bleak days were still ahead. In November the little ship *Fortune* arrived with thirty-five settlers but few supplies, so that the colony was burdened with thirty-five more mouths to feed. Winter was hard and crops the following summer were poor. The Pilgrims continued to pray, and they also tried to help themselves—by searching the woods for acorns and wild roots, by prowling the shores to gather clams and crabs.

By the summer of 1623 they were no better than skeletons wandering around in rags, when two more ships arrived with another ninety people to feed. But after a time a warm, gentle rain began to fall. The showers continued for weeks, and in the fields the drooping corn began to stand firm upon its green stalks. That fall the Pilgrims filled their bins with a plentiful harvest.

60

"THE HEAVENLY LAND"

Shrewd Peter Minuit buys Manhattan Island for a good price, but his successors fail to govern their new colony wisely.

When they saw that there were English settlements firmly planted in Virginia and New England, the Dutch again began to stir. Since 1609, when Henry Hudson had sailed his river in the *Half Moon,* they had been playing a game of hit-and-run in the New World. In 1611, two small trading vessels, the *Little Fox* and the *Little Crane,* became the first of many such ships that sailed into the bay and river that Hudson had discovered. After swapping trinkets for beaver pelts with the Indians, the voyagers seemed eager only to sail away. But Captain Adriaen Block was different. In 1613-14 this brave old sea dog discovered the Housatonic and Connecticut Rivers, Rhode Island, and Block Island.

Eight years later, the Dutch West India Company was chartered for the purpose of trading and colonizing in the areas Hudson and Block had claimed. The first settlers arrived in 1623—some thirty families of French-speaking Walloons from Holland. They were Huguenots (Protestants), and like the English Separatists they were unpopular at home and eager to find religious freedom in the New World. They were a restless group, even when making a new start in America. Some settled at Fort Nassau, the present site of Albany. Others settled on Governor's Island, and a few may have made their homes on that island which the Indians called Ma-na-hat-ta, meaning "Heavenly Land."

The first official Dutch settlement on Manhattan Island began three years later when, in May, the little ship *Zee Meeuw* sailed slowly into the harbor. Aboard her was shrewd Peter Minuit, who was empowered by the authorities in Amsterdam to buy the island from the Indians as a site for a Dutch colony. Minuit struck a bargain with the Indian chiefs, who gave him the land in exchange for trinkets worth sixty Dutch guilders (about $24 in our money).

The Dutch quickly established a settlement on the island, naming it New Amsterdam. A strong fort surrounded a colony of some thirty houses and two windmills. A fine sandy road ran along the shore, and across the water rose the wooded hills of Brooklyn. At the wharf was a crane used in unloading the boats from overseas, and

Minuit bought Manhattan Island from the Indians.

Peter Minuit

family, old and young, master and servant, black and white—nay, even the very cat and dog—enjoyed a community of privilege and each a right to a corner. Here the old burgher [master of the house] would sit in perfect silence, puffing his pipe, looking in the fire with half-shut eyes, and thinking of nothing for hours together; the goede vrouw [good wife] on the opposite side would employ herself diligently in spinning yarn or knitting stockings. The young folk would crowd around the hearth, listening with breathless attention to some old crone of a Negro who was the oracle of the family, and who, perched like a raven in a corner of the chimney, would croak forth for a long winter afternoon a string of incredible stories about New England witches, grisly ghosts, horses without heads, and hairbreadth escapes and bloody encounters among the Indians."

WEAKNESS OF DUTCH RULE

Cheerful though home life in New Amsterdam appeared, the Dutch were in trouble. The traders who organized the Dutch settlements in the New World simply could not bring themselves to give away land even in the wilderness. The poor were no better off in the New World than they had been in the Old. Then, too, the director-generals that were sent to run the colony were quarrelsome and highhanded. Peter Minuit, who had bargained his trinkets for Manhattan Island, was such a tricky fellow that he was soon out of a job, although that was not the last the New World would hear of him. Wouter Van Twiller, who replaced Minuit, was a conceited chap who lived like an oyster in a shell. William Kiefft, who followed Van Twiller, was an Amsterdam merchant who bungled in his dealings with the Indians and lost their friendship. But the greatest weakness of the Dutch was their inability to give the people any share in government.

here once a week the Dutch gathered for market day. An old trail, sloping up north of the fort, enabled travelers to see on all sides and thus learn if enemies were about. That trail is today known as Broadway. The little Dutch houses of black and yellow brick, each with its gabled roof, large front door, iron knocker, and numerous small windows were set in neat rows. Mops and brooms and scrubbing brushes seemed to be going all day long, for no Dutch woman could be happy unless her home shone with cleanliness. Washington Irving drew a splendid picture of life in New Amsterdam:

"As to the family, they always entered in at the gate, and most generally lived in the kitchen. . . . The fireplaces were of a truly patriarchal magnitude, where the whole

62

Neat rows of houses with gabled roofs marked the clean Dutch settlements in New York.

JOURNEY TO CONNECTICUT

*Unhappy with the religious practices
of the Puritans, groups of settlers march
through the wilderness to set up
new colonies.*

Where the Dutch through bungling and weakness, failed as colonizers, the English prospered. The Massachusetts Bay Company was organized in 1628 by a religious group called Puritans, and the following year five ships carried settlers to its first town at Salem. Seventeen ships, bringing more than a thousand new colonists, crossed the Atlantic during the next few months. Some settled in Charlestown, but others rowed to the peninsula across the Charles River and laid out the first streets of Boston. All through the 1630's, the British boom in colonizing continued. The names

of new towns began to dot the map of Massachusetts: Medford, Watertown, Roxbury, Dorchester, and Newtown (now Cambridge).

Conditions in England at the time were far from happy. If James I had seemed a stubborn, iron-willed king, Charles I, who followed him to the throne, was even more severe concerning the religious practices of the Puritans.

But when the Puritans reached the New World, they wished religious freedom only for those who thought as they thought and worshiped as they worshiped. Little groups, dissatisfied with the highhanded manners of their neighbors, struck off on their own, going north, south, and west, in search of homes.

Early in the 1630's more than 200 colonists from the Massachusetts towns of Watertown, Dorchester, and Newtown made the long, weary march to build new homes in the wilderness of Connecticut. These hardy pioneers, setting out on foot,

pushed through forests over narrow Indian paths. Women carried young children in their arms and drove the cattle ahead of them. The men lumbered forward like pack animals burdened down with firearms, ammunition, utensils, food. From Massachusetts to the pretty meadowlands along the Connecticut River, where they settled, was a journey of about fourteen days. The first colonists, led by William Holmes, reached Windsor in September, 1633. The following year another party under John Oldham settled at Wethersfield, and in 1635 Thomas Hooker brought a band of followers to Hartford.

Hammers pounded and saws buzzed as forts and houses sprang up along the banks of the Connecticut River. Fields were plowed and corn planted. Oiled paper covered the window openings in the first crude

The road to Connecticut was long and difficult, but many colonists were glad to take the risk.

dwellings. All the furniture had to be built by hand. The glow of the fireplace and burning pine knots gave the only light at night.

Yet these Britishers in Connecticut, knowing they were invading land first explored by Adriaen Block and claimed by the Dutch, were determined to work together and hold what they had taken. In 1637 they established the General Court, in which all the towns of Connecticut were represented so that they could act together in case of danger. It was not the Dutch they feared, but the Pequots, the most warlike Indian tribe in New England, who claimed Connecticut as part of their territory.

The leader of this hostile tribe of 3,000 Pequots was Sassacus, an intelligent young chief. He told his people that if the English were allowed to get a foothold in Connecticut, their land would be lost forever. About twenty years before, a trader named Thomas Hunt had sailed up the Connecticut River and had tricked twenty Indians

Hunt tricked twenty Pequots into boarding his ship, then sold them into slavery.

into boarding his boat with promises of presents. Instead, Hunt had carried them off to Spain and had sold them into slavery.

No Pequot had ever forgotten Hunt's treachery. It was an evil act that one day must be avenged. And Sassacus had other proof that no white person could be trusted: the cold-blooded murder of two old Indian chiefs in Massachusetts, and the slaying by a Dutch trader of Totabam, the chief of a small branch of the Pequot tribe. To the Pequots, the white man, with his terrible gunpowder, was an enemy who intended to grab all the land, kill all the animals in the forest, and turn all Indians into slaves.

The situation was not helped by the preaching of Puritan ministers, who spoke of the devil as someone who walked the earth. Anyone who, in the opinion of the Puritans, did not live by the "true" religion could be possessed by the devil. A person who smiled while a minister was preaching could be accused of dealing with the devil. Persons with squinty eyes could easily be branded as witches. Indians, who did not believe in the Puritan faith, were all children of the devil and, therefore, must be watched closely.

In July of 1636, John Oldham, the founder of Wethersfield, was murdered in his boat. In revenge the English burned Indian homes and cornfields. In the following months there were more deeds of violence. A settler named Butterfield was caught by the Indians while cutting hay in his meadow and burned at the stake. Three

Angry Pequots attacked the Connecticut settlers.

settlers, off hunting ducks, were brutally killed. Each incident added to the fear that crept through the English settlements in the Connecticut Valley.

On the night of April 22, 1637, a band of 200 Pequots sailed quietly up the river to Wethersfield. They hid their canoes in a small branch of the river and waited for daybreak. It was time for spring planting, and the men, women, and children of Wethersfield were out early that morning, working in their fields. All at once the Indians rushed from the bushes. Tomahawks and scalping knives flashed in the sunlight. The screams of the surprised settlers mingled with the wild yells of the Indians.

After killing some of the settlers at Wethersfield, the Indians made off with two girls.

67

Within minutes, the Indians were back in their canoes, shouting as they sailed down-river. With them were two girls they had captured. In the fields of Wethersfield lay the bodies of six men and three women. The survivors stared at the departing Indians, who waved aloft the clothes they had stripped from their victims. The two girls sat terror-stricken in the canoe. The older of them was only sixteen years of age.

In time, through the intervention of the Dutch, the girls were permitted to return home. They had proved a disappointment to the Pequots, who had hoped to learn from them the secret of making gunpowder. But the valley was now aroused. On May 1, at Hartford, the General Court decided to raise an army under an experienced military leader, Captain John Mason.

THE CONNECTICUT ARMY ADVANCES

On the morning of May 26, the little Connecticut army of seventy-seven men advanced upon the chief enemy fort at Pequot Hill in West Mystic. With them that day was Captain John Underhill, who left this account of the fighting:

"Our soldiers were shot, some through the shoulders, some in the face, some in the head, some in the legs. Captain Mason and myself lost each of us a man, and had near twenty wounded. Most courageously these Pequots behaved themselves. But seeing the fort was too hot for us, we devised a way how we might save ourselves. Captain Mason, entering into a wigwam, brought out a firebrand after he had many [of his soldiers] wounded in the house. Then he set fire on the west side, where he had entered. I set fire on the south end with a train of powder. The fires of both, meeting in the center of the fort, blazed most terribly, and burnt all in the space of half an hour....

68

"Many were burnt in the fort, both men, women, and children. Others forced [their way] out . . . twenty and thirty at a time, which our soldiers received and entertained with the point of the sword. Down fell men, women, and children. . . . It is reported that there were about four hundred souls in this fort, and not above five of them escaped out of our hands. . . ."

So for the first time Englishmen fought Indians for the land of America. But the men of Connecticut were satisfied. They had won the right to live as they pleased in the wilderness.

And they wasted little time in taking advantage of that right. Less than a year after

The Connecticut army of seventy-seven men stormed and set fire to the Pequot village.

the war with the Pequots ended, about 250 men, women, and children followed Theophilus Eaton, Edward Hopkins, and the Reverend John Davenport into Connecticut to found a colony at New Haven. The laws stating what these settlers could and could not do were printed in a pamphlet bound in blue covers, thus giving to the American language the term "blue laws." Some of the laws were:

"No one shall cross a river on Sunday but an authorized clergyman.

"No one shall run on the Sabbath day, or walk in his garden, except reverently to and from meeting [church].

"No woman shall kiss her child on the Sabbath or fasting day.

"No one shall travel, cook victuals [food], make beds, sweep houses, cut hair, or shave on the Sabbath day.

"Every male shall have his hair cut round according to a cap.

"A man who strikes his wife shall be fined $10.

"No one shall read common prayer, keep Christmas or saint days, make minced pies, dance, play cards, or play on any instrument of music, except the drum, trumpet, and Jew's-harp."

The blue laws allowed the people of New Haven little freedom, but elsewhere in Connecticut freedom was gaining. A sermon preached by Thomas Hooker at Hartford in 1638 led to the famous "Fundamental Orders." Adopted by the settlements of Windsor, Wethersfield, and Hartford, these orders said that "the foundation of authority is in the free consent of the people." In other words, only the people could say how they were to be governed.

The Fundamental Orders were Connecticut's first written constitution. They provided for a form of representative government, and the election of a governor and magistrates (judges). They limited terms of office and gave guarantees of equal representation and taxation.

69

PURITAN TROUBLEMAKER

Exiled from Massachusetts for speaking his mind too freely, Roger Williams founds his own colony in Rhode Island.

Roger Williams was a man of strong beliefs. Almost from the moment he reached Boston in early 1631, he was in trouble with the Puritan church rulers. A rebel who had fought for religious freedom in England, Williams went on fighting in America. Like a shuttlecock, he bounced from town to town—from Boston to Salem to the Plymouth colony and back to Salem.

As much as any one person could, Williams soon had Massachusetts in an uproar. Did a court have the right to punish a person who refused to follow the religious customs as ordered by the clergy? Indeed, it had no such right, said Williams. In matters of religion "man is responsible to God alone!" Did the king of England have the right to give away land belonging to the Indians? Indeed, the king had no such right, said Williams. He believed that no one should settle in America unless he purchased the land from the original Indian owners. Did the church have the right to run the political life of a settlement? Indeed, it had no such right, said Williams.

Roger Williams was a handsome man, and everyone found him gentle and charming—when he was not arguing for his beliefs. He refused to keep them to himself, and the General Court banished him from Massachusetts in the winter of 1635-36.

Cheerful and determined, he set off on the "narrow Indian path" out of Salem to found his own colony in Rhode Island. In the spring he reached the west bank of the Seekonk River, paid the Indians a fair price for the land he wanted, and in gratitude for "God's providence" in bringing

Roger Williams

him safely to this place, named his settlement Providence. Under the wise administration of Roger Williams, the colonists of Rhode Island prospered and other settlements sprang up at Portsmouth, Newport, and Warwick.

In Rhode Island no one was placed in the stocks, as had happened in Massachusetts, for failing to attend church regularly. In Rhode Island no one was whipped, as had happened to one planter in Massachusetts, for saying he would rather hear a dog bark than the minister preach. In Rhode Island no one was dipped in the public pond, as happened in Massachusetts, for whispering in church. In Rhode Island anyone could hold whatever religious beliefs he wished, as long as he behaved "peaceably and quietly."

Another colony that grew out of the search for freedom of religion was Maryland. In England, where the Roman Catholic Church was outlawed, Lord Baltimore dreamed of establishing a colony in the New World which would allow Roman Catholics to worship in their own way. The old nobleman died before he could see his dream come true. But his son carried out his plan, and in the spring of 1634, two little ships reached Chesapeake Bay with the first settlers of Maryland. Of the some 200 gentlemen-adventurers, yeomen, artisans, laborers, and servants who crowded the decks of the *Ark* and the *Dove,* less than half were Catholics. Catholic and Protestant would have to live side by side in peace if the colony were to succeed.

THE FIRST GENERAL ASSEMBLY

The settlers soon struck a bargain with the Yoacomico Indians. In exchange for axes, hatchets, farm tools, and bolts of cloth, they received an entire village, which they renamed St. Mary's City. A statehouse was built, and within a year the first general assembly met. In England the laws

Churches were among the first buildings to be put up in the New World.

passed by the colonists were quickly vetoed. But the laws sent over from England were as quickly rejected by the colonists. By 1638 the backers of the Maryland company agreed that the people had a right to self-government.

Meanwhile Catholic and Protestant, living together in Maryland, set an example of how well religious tolerance could work. In 1649 the General Assembly passed an "Act Concerning Religion" which imposed fines and even punishment by flogging if any Christian was disturbed because of his religion. Earlier a Catholic member of the Governor's Council had taken away the key to a Protestant chapel, but the authorities had moved quickly and fined him 500 pounds of tobacco. When the tobacco was sold, the money was to be used for the support of a Protestant minister.

LIFE IN A CHANGING AMERICA

Farms and villages grow and prosper as colonists from several lands settle in the New World.

Early in 1631, the Dutch founded a settlement in present-day Delaware, near Lewes (pronounced Lewis). They called it Zwannendael, or "Valley of Swans." The Dutch quickly managed to get themselves killed. A tin coat of arms of Holland, nailed to a post, started the trouble. A young Indian chief took the tin plate, wishing to fashion it into a bowl for his pipe. Both the Indians and the Dutch lost their tempers, and when the next Dutch ship arrived at Zwannendael, all that remained was the ruins of houses that had been burned to the ground.

Back into the New World now came Peter Minuit, the man who had bought Manhattan Island. He had organized a colonizing venture for a newcomer in America —Sweden. Minuit's first party of Swedish settlers reached Delaware in 1638, building Fort Christina on the site of present-day Wilmington. Twelve more expeditions were sent from Sweden in the following years. From the start the Swedes were wise colonizers, who scarcely ever spoke a harsh word to the Indians. The Indians watched with admiration as the Swedes brought a new type of dwelling into the wilderness— the log cabin. The hard-working Swedes built mills, houses, boats, and wharves, and set up shops for barrelmaking, brewing, baking, and weaving. In 1640 they shouted a joyous welcome to Reorus Torkillus, the first Lutheran clergyman in America.

The first log cabins in America were built by Swedish colonists along the Delaware River.

THE POPULATION GROWS

By then any sea captain who was an old hand at sailing the Atlantic must have blinked in wonder at how greatly the New World had changed in the last ten years. The Dutch on Manhattan Island and the Swedes on the shores of the Delaware were only a handful of settlers compared to the number of English who came to the New World in the "Great Migration" of 1630 to 1640. In Massachusetts the population of the English was estimated at 14,000. English settlers elsewhere were believed to number 8,000 in Virginia, 2,000 in Connecticut, 300 in Rhode Island, 1,500 in the combined areas of New Hampshire and Maine, and 1,500 in Maryland.

By 1650, the growing population of the English in North America was estimated at 52,000. Ten years later English and Dutch settlers numbered 85,000. In 1671, Governor Berkeley estimated the population of Virginia at 45,000, including 6,000 white servants and 2,000 Negro slaves. Twenty years later, Boston alone claimed 7,000 inhabitants; Newport, Rhode Island, 2,600; New York City (Dutch New Amsterdam) 3,900; Philadelphia 4,000; and Charleston, South Carolina, 1,100.

The settlers' first houses were made of boards driven into the ground like the palings of a fence and contained only a single room. Roofs, slanting front and back, were made of thatch. Chimneys were constructed from branches woven together and plastered with mud or clay. The danger of fire was great, for the heat dried the mud and clay,

New Englanders held that schooling was important.

causing it to fall off and expose the branches to flying sparks. The problem was not solved until limestone beds in Maine and Rhode Island made the use of mortar possible.

HOME LIFE IN AMERICA

As a family prospered, it added rooms for sleeping. About 1650, with the development of an iron industry, hand-wrought nails began to take the place of wooden pegs. Cabinetmakers were kept busy turning out chairs, chests, spinning wheels, and tables, and there were few colonial homes that did not have one high-back chair used by the "head of the family" as a sign of his authority. A wife might stand, or sit on a stool, while her husband settled comfortably in his chair, a king in his own castle.

As early as 1642, the General Court in

Massachusetts passed a law that required every parent to teach his children to read and to practice at least one trade. Another law, five years later, required every township of fifty families to support a school that could teach children reading and writing. Each township of one hundred families was required to provide a grammar school that could prepare students for college. Harvard College, founded in 1636, was at the time the only college in the colonies.

THE FIRST PRINTING PRESS

The first printing press in the English colonies was set up by Stephen Day in Cambridge in 1639, and the following year the *Bay Psalm Book* became the first book published in America. But the book New England boys and girls studied most was the *New England Primer*. This included such sections as a "Rhymed Alphabet," and "Dialogue between Christ, Youth, and the Devil." Typical verses in the "Rhymed Alphabet" read:

N   *Noah did view*
    The old World and new.
O   *Young Obadias,*
    David, Josias,
    All were pious.
P   *Peter deny'd*
    His Lord and cry'd.

Boston's first bookstore was opened in 1652, and four years later the city established the first public library. During the growing season, the tasks of farming filled the days of the great majority of people. Even children were expected to do their share of the family work. The colonial planter learned to grow three crops in a field, first harvesting his corn, then using the stalks as poles for his beans and permitting the vines of his pumpkins to spread among the hills of his corn.

Other crops introduced by the English into New England were cabbages, turnips, onions, carrots, and parsnips. The Dutch brought to the New World its first beets, spinach, endive, leeks, and herbs like parsley and dill. The Germans in Pennsylvania introduced asparagus, and the Swedes probably brought the first peaches. Wheat, a failure in Plymouth, could be grown with great success along the Connecticut Valley, which became the main wheat and cereal raising center in the colonies by the early 1650's.

EARLY INDUSTRIES

Americans begin to manufacture goods that once had to be brought from Europe.

The first ironworks in America was set up in 1619 on Falling Creek in Virginia, and by the middle of the 1640's ironworks were operating in Massachusetts at Saugus and Braintree. Among the important craftsmen in every village was the blacksmith, who turned out the chains and plows, the axheads and scythe blades, the hoes, pitchforks, and sickles on which the farmer depended. From his shop also came the popular two-wheeled cart.

Other industries sprang up. Maine's first sawmill was operating near York in 1623, and that same year New Hampshire had its first salt works near Piscataqua. Three years later the Dutch at New Amsterdam gave America its first flour mill. In 1629 the first colonial brick kiln was built in Salem and the first New England tannery was set up at Lynn, Massachusetts. Four years later Dorchester had the first water mill for grinding corn. By 1641 Salem had added a glass factory to its industries, and in 1643 twenty families of skilled cloth workers from Yorkshire, England, settled in Rowley, Massachusetts, and opened a woolen mill.

75

All along the New England coastline, shipyards were set up to build ships for trading or fishing.

From 1624, when a ship carpenter arrived in Plymouth, shipbuilding played a large part in the life of New England. Boats were needed for fishing, which was itself a major industry, and New England was soon producing its own special kind of vessel known as a shallop. This craft was a simple boat, fitted with both oars and a sail, and almost any boy handy with tools could make one. But ships of greater size were built as well. *The Blessing of the Bay,* a thirty-ton sloop, was launched in 1631, and "a prodigious ship of 300 tons"—almost twice the size of the *Mayflower*—was launched at Salem in 1641. By 1665 it was estimated that 1,300 boats were fishing regularly off the Grand Banks of Newfoundland, while another 300 ships from New England traded in every port of North America and Europe.

ROADS AND MAIL

The "narrow Indian path" that Roger Williams followed out of Salem in 1636 when he set off to found Rhode Island was probably no more than eighteen inches wide. Indians always traveled in single file and their trails through the wilderness were narrow ribbons of beaten-down grass. A white man's road was usually a rod (16½ feet) wide, and the work of cutting trees and clearing rocks to build it was a backbreaking job. Even so, in 1639 the General Court in Massachusetts ordered every town to lay out roads connecting it with the next town.

That same year the first "post office" was established in Massachusetts when the General Court selected the home of Richard Fairbanks in Boston as the place where all letters were to be deposited. In 1658 a Virginia law provided that planters must forward a letter from plantation to plantation until it reached its destination. A fine of 350 pounds of tobacco was imposed on any planter who failed to do so.

Governor Francis Lovelace of New York proposed a relay of "post riders" between New York City and Boston in 1673, with a trip to be completed each way once every month. After a few journeys, however, the system was dropped. Four years later the General Court of Massachusetts appointed John Hayward of Boston the first official letter carrier in America. He performed his duties so well that upon his death the job was given to his son.

COLONIAL MONEY

Each colony used its own chief product for money. New York accepted beaver skins in payment for debts, Rhode Island wool, and South Carolina rice. Virginia permitted fines to be paid in tobacco. Indian wampum was also accepted at the rate of three black beads or six white beads for a penny, and the fact that the Indians would accept glass beads for money helped to develop the glass industry. The first mint was estab-

lished in Boston in 1652. John Hull, a silversmith, was authorized by Massachusetts to turn out the Pine Tree shilling, a crude silver coin about the size of a half dollar. A coin accepted throughout the colonies was the Spanish dollar or "piece of eight." Sometimes this coin was called a "bit of eight," explaining why to this day we refer to a twenty-five cent piece as "two bits."

TWO LITTLE WARS

One-legged Peter Stuyvesant thunders against the British, but finally has to give in to the might of the British fleet.

The last director-general of New Amsterdam—and its best—was rawboned, leathery-faced old Peter Stuyvesant. He stomped around on a wooden leg and was called, behind his back, "Peter the Headstrong." In 1655, the Swedes seized a Dutch trading post on the Delaware River at New Castle. Stuy-

Fiery, headstrong Peter Stuyvesant tried to keep New Amsterdam Dutch, but finally had to give up to the British, who changed its name to New York.

vesant's voice, which sounded as though it came out of a barrel, could now be heard the length of Manhattan Island. He collected a fleet of seven stout sailing ships and set out to teach the Swedes a lesson.

The "war" was over almost before it began, and to the credit of the victorious Dutch, the region prospered under their control. They rebuilt New Amstel (New Castle) into a full-fledged town, greatly increased the trade in furs, and encouraged farming. If they governed in their usual highhanded way, at least they were tolerant of Swedish religious customs.

But unhappy days were ahead for New Amsterdam and headstrong Peter. The English in Connecticut were looking enviously at the Dutch holdings along the Hudson River. They followed the advice of the governor of Connecticut to keep "crowding the

Dutch out of those places where they have occupied, but without hostility or any act of violence." Each year more and more Englishmen moved into New Amsterdam. The Dutch, who were peace-loving traders at heart, tried to get along with their English neighbors, but commercial jealousies between England and the Netherlands brought trouble. The first Anglo-Dutch War (1652-54) was a hit-and-run affair that ended in a patched-up peace which lasted ten years. In 1664 the two countries were snarling at each other again, and in late August of that year four British warships appeared off New Amsterdam and demanded its surrender.

Old Peter Stuyvesant thrust two large pistols in his belt and called for a brave defense. His council listened, squirmed at the thought of bloodshed, and then left the meeting (or so Washington Irving declared) "dodging through narrow lanes and alleys, staring at every little dog that barked, mistaking lamp posts for British grenadiers."

Stuyvesant pounded his wooden leg and called for action, but the Dutch only nailed up their doors to keep out the terrible British. They surrendered New Amsterdam "without a blow or a tear."

The English turned out to be mild rather than terrible. They did change the names of settlements, so that New Amsterdam became New York and Beverwyck became Albany. The story Washington Irving told of Stuyvesant stomping off to his farm, turning his high-back chair so he would never have to look at the captured city, and cutting down the English cherry trees in his yard was a good tale, but untrue. No better friends could be found on Manhattan Island than old Peter and Governor Richard Nicolls, the man to whom he had surrendered the city. Each dined often at the other's home. And in the same spirit the colonial Dutch and English went on living together peaceably and comfortably.

Briefly, in 1673, with the outbreak of another little war between England and the Netherlands, the Dutch recaptured New York. But when a peace treaty was signed the following year, they gave the city back to the English. After this, the chief worry of New York's Dutch and English was the pirates who were making the city a favorite hangout. The Blue Boar Tavern, on the outskirts of the city, rang with their wild shouts, songs, and fights. Here rough-looking rascals paraded about in fine colored waistcoats and feathered hats, with cutlass and pistols hanging from the sashes around their middles. Whoever saw them had to admit that there was something new in the New World.

WILLIAM PENN COMES TO AMERICA

Unable to practice their religion in England, the Quakers cross the Atlantic to taste the freedom of the New World.

It was around 1647 that a new religious group, the Society of Friends, began to gain a following in England. They were also known as Quakers. The founder of the movement was George Fox, the son of a weaver and a shoemaker by training. Young Fox wandered through England, seeking a minister in whose preaching he could be-

The Blue Boar Tavern was a pirates' hangout.

lieve. Simply because a clergyman had been educated at Oxford or Cambridge University, Fox decided, was no guarantee that he had found God. And simply because men erected a building with their own hands and called it a church was no guarantee that the spirit of God dwelt there. Then one day George Fox was struck by a joyous thought. The true "temple of God" was in the heart of each man.

Questioning the right of the educated clergymen of England to speak for God, scorning their elaborate churches was bad enough. But the Quakers went even further. They said that since God lived within each man, it was nonsense to divide people into "ruling" and "lower" classes. God loved all people, and the Quakers addressed everyone as "thee" and "thou" to show that they considered them to be friends. The ruling class of England soon let the Quakers know that they were not wanted.

PERSECUTION OF THE QUAKERS

When the first Quakers reached Boston in 1656, they were thrown into prison and banished from Massachusetts without trial. That same year Connecticut passed a law imposing fines and banishment from the colony upon all members of the Society of Friends, and Puritan clergymen in New England preached sermons upon "the Devil, Quakers and Indians."

The Dutch were just as harsh toward the Quakers. Five Friends arrived in New Amsterdam in 1657. Peter Stuyvesant ordered them severely punished and banished them to Rhode Island. The following year, the New England Confederation, which spoke for the Bay Colony, Plymouth, and New Haven, ordered the Quakers out of all three colonies and threatened them with death if they returned. In 1660 a Quaker named Mary Dyer defied this law and came back to Boston where she was hanged.

81

But the Quakers would not give up their beliefs, and in 1664 they managed to buy land for a settlement in New Jersey. Meanwhile, in England, William Penn was working for their cause. Penn was an aristocrat, the son of an admiral. While a student at Oxford University, he became a Quaker, shocking his father. Oxford expelled Penn and the admiral sent him on a tour of Europe, hoping that a change of scene would help him to mend his ways.

The result was just the opposite. Penn soon wanted to change everything—religion, government, social manners, and customs. He was sentenced to jail, but it had no effect. He went on preaching his ideas to anyone who would listen and writing pamphlets for anyone who would read them. He traveled through Holland and Germany, winning new converts for the Quakers.

When Penn's father died, King Charles II owed him 16,000 pounds. In payment of this debt, the king gave Penn a royal grant to establish a colony in America. Now at last Penn could put his beliefs into practice. He wrote his famous letter to the Indians, assuring them that when he came to his new colony—Pennsylvania—he wished "to enjoy it with your [the Indians'] love and consent."

He admitted that other colonists had committed injustices against the Indians and caused "the shedding of blood." He added: "But I am not such a man, as is well known in my own country. I have great love towards you, and I desire to win and gain your love and friendship by a kind, just and peaceable life, and the people I send are of the same mind, and shall in all things behave themselves accordingly." He promised that if any inhabitant of his colony should act unfairly against any Indian, he would be speedily tried before a jury of six white persons and six Indians.

Penn spent weeks working out a plan of government for his colony. "Government seems to me a part of religion itself," he said. There were three common ideas of government: "monarchy, aristocracy and democracy, the rule of one, a few and many." For his own government he chose the principle that "any government is free to the people under it" where "the laws rule, and the people are a party to those laws." Again Penn declared: "Let men be good, and the government cannot be bad." Under Penn's plan, there would be guarantees for religious freedom, trial by jury, fair practices between whites and Indians, and payment to the Indians for the land.

Penn's ideas of government brought to America a belief in human decency and dignity. Every man should be free to say and think what he pleased. Every man was a king in his own home. All the people should take part in making and enforcing the laws. A great nation, Penn said, must be a nation of good morals. The laws he framed for his colony forbade corruption, fraud, bribery, extortion, and slander. They also forbade offenses against God, such as swearing, lying, drunkenness, duels, bearbaiting, and cockfights. They forbade anything "which excites the people to rudeness, cruelty, looseness and irreligion."

WILLIAM PENN FOUNDS A QUAKER COLONY IN THE NEW WORLD

Indians and white settlers alike stood cheering at the water's edge when William Penn landed at New Castle, Delaware, in October of 1682. The very next day he announced that the first court would be held in New Castle in early November. There was to be no delay in beginning his colony on a basis of justice for all. Nor did Penn long delay in dealing with the Indians. Under an elm at Shackamaxon (now part of Philadelphia), he met with chiefs of the Leni Lenapes, the Susquehannocks, and the Shawnees to work out a "treaty of purchase and amity." He was a Quaker, Penn told the Indians, and his religion would not allow him to use "hostile weapons" against them. He had come to America "not to injure others but to do good."

Philadelphia, the capital of Penn's new province, grew quickly. By the end of 1684, it had 357 completed houses and a population of about 2,500.

The Quakers lived peacefully with the Swedes, Finns, and Dutch, the earlier settlers in the region. The people were industrious and developed trade with the other colonies and the West Indies. Shipbuilding soon became an important business. By 1685 Penn's colony had 7,000 inhabitants, and there was a new settlement at Germantown. Five years later William Rittenhouse built America's first paper mill on a branch of Wissahickon Creek. The new community, digging its roots into the wilderness, was busy and prosperous.

But the real strength of Penn's colony was the example it gave to America of how well a true democracy could work.

Under an elm at Shackamaxon, Penn offered the Indians a treaty of peace.

FLOATING DOWN THE MISSISSIPPI

Father Jacques Marquette and Louis Joliet, followed by La Salle, explore the heart of the new continent for France.

Having lost out in the Iroquois country, because of Champlain's blunder, the French pushed westward and explored the lands bordering the Great Lakes. Here they built forts and trading posts that gave them control of these inland seas. Mackinac and Sault Ste. Marie made the French masters of the junctions of Lakes Huron, Michigan, and

Superior, and Fort Radisson protected the far end of Lake Superior. Doggedly the French forged a chain around the inland empire they were building. Fort Frontenac rose on the shores of Lake Ontario. Fort Niagara guarded the passage to Lake Erie. When Detroit was founded in 1701, the French controlled the connection between Lake Erie and Lake Huron.

Jesuit fathers in black robes carried their religion to the Indians of mid-America and revealed to the world new wonders of the wilderness. Father Louis Hennepin was the first white man to look upon mighty Niagara Falls. Stringing their missions deeper into the lake country, the Jesuits heard of a mysterious and mighty river to the

south—the Mississippi. No river was quite so great and majestic as this one, the Indians said. Father Jacques Marquette had been in North America seven years when he decided to find this wonderful river. With him on his journey went his good-humored friend, the explorer Louis Joliet.

"We joyfully plied our paddles," wrote Father Marquette of the beginning of that brave adventure in May of 1673. The first Indians they visited were friendly Menominees, who tried to persuade them not to make the trip. "They represented to me that I would meet nations who never show mercy to strangers, but break their heads without any cause," Marquette later recalled. The Indians spoke of monsters that lived in the river and could eat men and canoes together. They spoke of a demon that swallowed all who dared to approach it, and of a country where the heat was so great it could cause death. Father Marquette said he was not afraid. He had been called to carry on God's work and believed he could defend himself against river monsters.

DOWN THE WISCONSIN RIVER

Father Marquette and his small party of seven Frenchmen traveled in two canoes. In early June they were paddling down the Wisconsin River. Vine-covered islands dotted the river. Great forests of oak, walnut, and basswood trees came down to the water's edge. They saw many deer and a place that looked like an iron mine. On they paddled, past forests, prairies, and hills, until on June 17 they reached the Mississippi.

On June 25 they visited a village of Illinois Indians on the west bank of the river. A man standing with his hand stretched toward the sun called a greeting: "How beautiful is the sun, O Frenchman, when thou comest to visit us! All our town awaits thee."

Father Marquette gave the Indians gifts and spoke of God as their Creator. The sachem of the tribe thanked Marquette, whom he addressed as "Blackgown." The sachem said:

"Never has the earth been so beautiful, nor the sun so bright, as today. Never has our river been so calm, nor so free from rocks, which your canoes have removed as they passed. Never has our tobacco had so fine a flavor, nor our corn appeared so beautiful as we behold it today. Here is my son, that I give thee, that thou mayest know my heart. I pray thee to take pity on me and my nation. Thou knowest the Great Spirit who has made us all. Thou speakest to him and

Father Jacques Marquette together with Louis Joliet reached the Mississippi River in 1673. 85

Father Jacques Marquette

Father Marquette and his companion Joliet paddled their canoes to the mouth of the Arkansas River, where the Indians told them they were only ten days' journey from the sea (that is, the Gulf of Mexico). In typical Indian fashion, the Arkansas tribesmen spent the entire day feasting. Father Marquette described their life in the Arkansas wilderness:

"These Indians are very courteous and liberal of what they have, but they are very poorly off for food, not daring to go and hunt the wild cattle [buffalo], for fear of their enemies. It is true, they have Indian corn in abundance, which they sow at all seasons. We saw some ripe, more just sprouting, and more just in ear, so that they sow hearest his word. Ask him to give me life and health, and come and dwell with us, that we may know him."

Afterward Marquette, Joliet, and their French boatmen were entertained at a feast. The Indians served a dish of corn meal boiled in water "and seasoned with grease," which they fed to their guests by the spoonful, as sometimes a small child is fed. Fish and roasted wild ox also were served, as well as "a large dog, which they had just killed, but learning that we did not eat it, it was withdrawn."

The Illinois village contained about 300 wigwams. As Father Marquette's party was shown through the streets, a man went before them, shouting in a loud voice that the palefaced visitors were not to be harmed. Again the Indians spoke of savage tribes that lived to the south and begged the white men to turn back while they were still safe. Again Father Marquette replied that he must trust in God to protect them.

three crops a year. They cook it in large earthen pots, which are very well made. They have also plates of baked earth, which they employ for various purposes.

"The men go naked, and wear their hair very short. They have their nose and ears pierced, and beads hanging from them. The women are dressed in wretched skins. They braid their hair in two plaits, which fall behind their ears. They have no ornaments to decorate their persons. . . . They serve their meats in large dishes, and everyone eats as much as he pleases, and they give the rest to one another. Their language is extremely difficult and with all my efforts, I could not succeed in pronouncing some words.

Louis Joliet

Wherever they went in the New World, Marquette and Joliet were welcomed by the Indians.

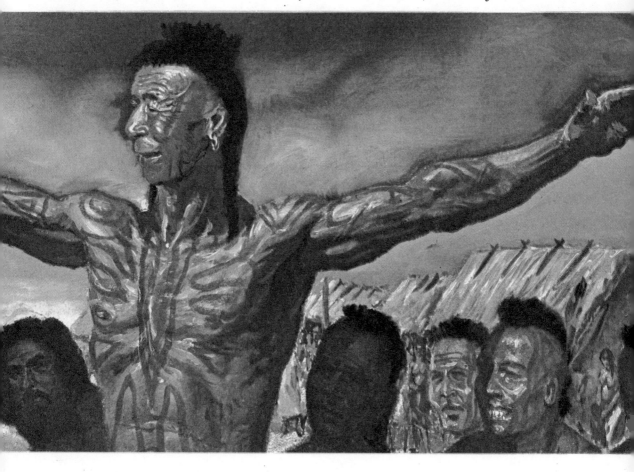

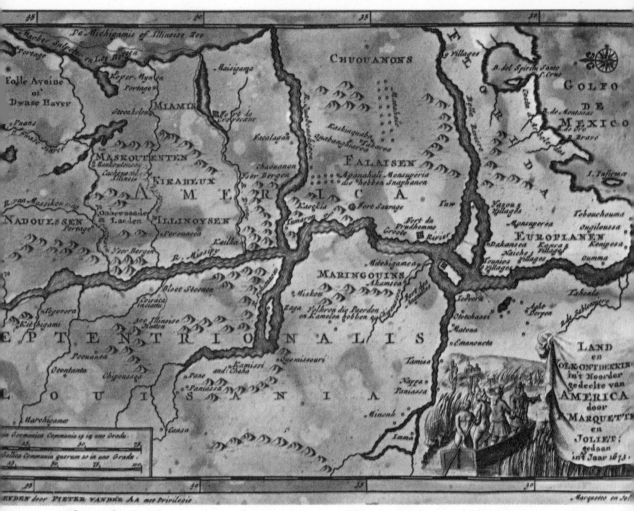

This early Dutch map shows the Mississippi and the land discovered by Marquette and Joliet.

"Their cabins, which are long and wide, are made of bark. They sleep at the two extremities [ends], which are raised about two feet from the ground. They keep their corn in large baskets, made of cane, or in gourds as large as half barrels. They do not know what a beaver is, their riches consisting in the hides of wild cattle. They never see snow, and know the winter only by the rain which falls oftener than in summer. They eat no fruit but watermelons. If they knew how to cultivate their ground, they might have plenty of all kinds."

Satisfied that they had learned the true course of the mighty Mississippi, Marquette, Joliet, and their boatmen turned their canoes homeward. They took a shorter route by way of the Illinois, Des Plaines,

and Chicago Rivers, and thus reached Lake Michigan, the "lake of the Illinois." Here at the water's edge Father Marquette baptized a dying child and that moment repaid him for all the weary days the trip had taken. He walked now on land where one day a great city would rise. Its name would be Chicago.

These inland explorations made by Marquette and Joliet were a beginning that no Frenchman could forget. The Spanish, the English, the Dutch, and others had nibbled at the fringes of North America, but the real discoverers of the continent were the French. They had been deep into this wilderness, they had floated on the great river that linked "the Frozen Sea and New Mexico," and now they dreamed of using that river to win a vast empire in the midlands of America. Among them was Robert Cavelier, Sieur de la Salle, who was determined to carry the flag of France down the Mississippi River to the sea.

La Salle was an explorer who had imagination as well as courage. He founded Fort Niagara and built the forty-ton *Griffon*, the first ship of any size to sail on the Great Lakes. In 1680 he established Fort Crèvecoeur (now Peoria) in Illinois and Fort Miami (now St. Joseph) in Michigan.

But La Salle's real triumph came when, on April 9, 1682, he reached the mouth of the Mississippi. He gathered his party on high ground and planted a cross bearing the arms of France. Shouts, volleys of muskets, and the chants of priests rang out as La Salle took possession of all the country. He gave it the name of Louisiana, in honor of the king of France. La Salle claimed not only the territory that the French had already explored, but also all the lands drained by the tributaries of the Mississippi, and a large part of the coast of the Gulf of Mexico.

To protect his new empire, La Salle built Fort Prudhomme on the Arkansas River at Chickasaw Bluffs and Fort St. Louis on the Illinois at Starved Rock. He formed the Indian tribes of Illinois into a federation, then sailed to France to seek permission to establish a settlement at the mouth of the Mississippi. In 1687, some 200 soldiers, mechanics, and colonists with him returned to the New World. That was too small a number to send into a country already occupied by the Spanish. Besides, the soldiers did not know how to fight, nor the seamen how to sail their ships, the mechanics how to handle their tools, the settlers how to get along in a wilderness.

La Salle put up a cross at the mouth of the Mississippi and claimed the land for France.

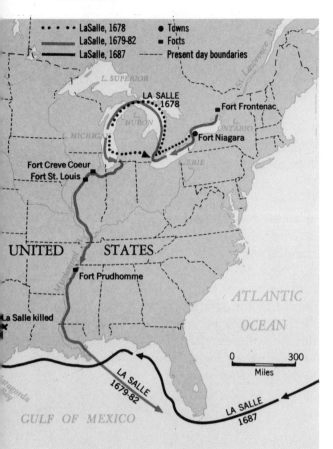

Map legend:
• • • • LaSalle, 1678　　● Towns
LaSalle, 1679-82　　■ Forts
LaSalle, 1687　　---- Present day boundaries

L. SUPERIOR

LA SALLE 1678

Fort Frontenac

L. HURON

L. MICHIGAN

Fort Niagara

L. ONTARIO

L. ERIE

Fort Creve Coeur
Fort St. Louis

UNITED　STATES

Fort Prudhomme

ATLANTIC

OCEAN

La Salle killed

0　　300
Miles

LA SALLE
1679-82

LA SALLE
1687

GULF OF MEXICO

Explorations of La Salle. The boundaries shown are those of the present day.

FRANCE LOSES INTEREST

Everything went wrong. The ships were far off course when finally they reached Matagorda Bay on the coast of Texas. Quarrels arose, and La Salle was ambushed and murdered by two members of his party.

Yet if France lost interest in her new possessions after that, no one was more at fault than La Salle. He had told only his closest friends about his explorations. So little was known in France about the lands he had discovered that people began to doubt their existence. Some said that La Salle had never actually reached the mouth of the Mississippi. Others said that the river simply disappeared into a hole in the ground.

In time, of course, France again became interested in the vast Louisiana Territory. **90** A French expedition under Pierre Le Moyne, Sieur d'Iberville, sailed into Mobile Bay in February, 1698. Journeying overland to the mouth of the Mississippi, Iberville led his party upstream. He reached the site of New Orleans in March of 1699, killed a buffalo, and erected a cross.

Although Iberville traveled as far north as Baton Rouge, he failed to discover the fortune in gold that the French king, Louis XIV, wanted. Once again the interest of the French faded. But Catholic missionaries and traders kept their claim to the country alive. A dozen years or so later, the French tried to make the Louisiana Territory an important part of their world empire.

JUST A BEGINNING

In roughly two hundred years much has been done—but great events are yet to come.

In round figures, 200 years had passed since Columbus had landed upon the shore of San Salvador, not knowing that he had stumbled upon a new world. First England, then France (and, to a lesser degree, the Dutch and the Swedes) had challenged Spain's claims to half the world. Already many mysteries of the wilderness had been solved. Already a new spirit had risen in this land of mighty rivers and lakes and mountains. People had begun to talk of their *right* to share in their government, their *right* to worship God in their own way, their *right* to a full and happy life.

Yet, really, the story of America was just beginning. It was like a river that starts as a little mountain brook and becomes mightier as it flows on. Many hardships and sacrifices and terrible conflicts lay ahead, and even now there were signs of what was to come. In 1688, the Quakers, meeting in Germantown, Pennsylvania, issued the first written statement in America that pro-

Homes were springing up all over the new land, and settlements soon followed them.

tested against human slavery. The following year New Hampshire was torn by King William's War. This was the first of the French and Indian wars that for many years would bring bloodshed to the colonies as France fought England for possession of the vast continent of North America.

There were other events, too, of a quite different kind. In 1690 a single printed sheet, *Publick Occurrences,* appeared in Boston. It was America's first newspaper—although a second issue was never printed. In 1693, Virginia gave the colonies a second institution of higher learning with the founding of William and Mary College, and eight years later Yale College was founded at Saybrook, Connecticut.

By 1700 the population of the colonies was estimated at 262,000, but everyone knew that the New World had just begun to grow. About this time there appeared in London a pamphlet written by Gabriel Thomas, one of the early settlers of Pennsylvania. He told of his life in the colonies where wages were high, taxes low, and work plentiful, where Chesapeake ducks and Pennsylvania cheesecake were the finest in the world. Only beautiful children were born in America, and they were "better natured, milder and more tender-hearted than those born in England."

Of course, there were Londoners who called the proud Pennsylvanian an out-and-out liar trying to trick people into coming to his wretched wilderness. But there were many who did believe him, and they did indeed make the long journey to America, seeking a better life in a new land.

91

VOLUME

2

THE INDIAN WARS

Volume II, The Indian Wars, *describes the
growth of the colonies in America and the battles
the settlers fought against the wilderness,
against Indians, and against tyranny.
In the century 1675-1775, the British defeated the
French in the French and Indian War and gained control
of more than half of North America. But the colonists
objected to "taxation without representation"
and there was bad feeling between them and
the mother country. A British ship was blown up in
Rhode Island, a massacre and a "tea party" took place
in Boston, and men began talking seriously of
human rights and of revolution.*

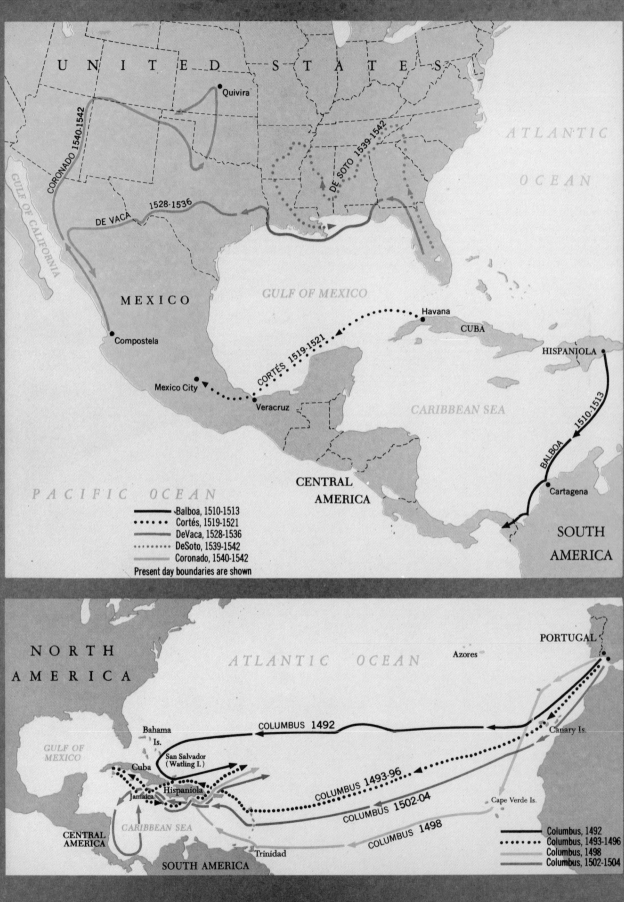